Matilda

Text copyright © 2008 Long Tail Books
Matilda © 1988 Quentin Blake

이 책에 사용된 일러스트레이션 사용 권한은 AP Watt Ltd를 통해 계약한 BOOKHOUSE Publishers에 있습니다.
한국 내에서 보호받는 저작물이므로 무단 전재와 무단 복제를 금합니다.

Contents

원서 읽는 단어장 소개 · 4
이 책의 구성 · 6
영어 원서 읽기 전문가가 대답해주는 FAQ · · · · · · · · · · · 10

Chapter 1-4
Comprehension Quiz · 14
Build Your Vocabulary · 22
Crossword Puzzle · 34

Chapter 5-8
Comprehension Quiz · 36
Build Your Vocabulary · 44
Crossword Puzzle · 56

Chapter 9-12
Comprehension Quiz · 58
Build Your Vocabulary · 66
Crossword Puzzle · 82

Chapter 13-16
Comprehension Quiz · 84
Build Your Vocabulary · 92
Crossword Puzzle · 106

Chapter 17-21
Comprehension Quiz · 108
Build Your Vocabulary · 116
Crossword Puzzle · 124

Answers
Comprehension Quiz Answers · · · · · · · · · · · · · · · · 128
Crossword Puzzle Answers · · · · · · · · · · · · · · · · · · · 130

 원서 읽는 단어장 소개

누구나 추천하는 최고의 영어 공부법, 영어 원서 읽기!

최근 영어 원서 읽기가 영어 공부법으로 주목받고 있습니다. 영어를 많이 접하는 것이 영어 실력을 향상시키는 가장 바람직한 방법이라는 공감대가 형성되면서, 쉽고 저렴하게 영어를 접할 수 있는 '원서 읽기'가 그 대안으로 각광받고 있는 것이지요.

실제로도 영어 좀 한다는 사람들이 원서 읽기를 추천하거나 어린 아이들이 엄마표 영어 연수 등을 통해 원서를 읽는 많은 사례들을 인터넷 상에서 쉽게 찾아볼 수 있습니다.

원서 읽기를 위한 최고의 친구, 『원서 읽는 단어장』!!

원서가 좋은 영어 공부 수단이긴 하지만, 한 번쯤 원서를 읽어본 독자들은 대부분 다음과 같은 고민을 하곤 합니다.

> 누가 여기 나오는 단어 좀 찾아주면 안되나?
> 모르는 단어가 나올 때마다 사전을 찾을 수도 없고,
> 그렇다고 그냥 지나치자니 뭔가 찜찜한데…
>
> 지금 내가 제대로 읽고 이해하고 있는 걸까?
> 번역된 책을 찾아서 일일이 대조할 수도 없고,
> 뭔가 확인할 방법이 있었으면 좋겠는데…

이런 문제를 해결해주고자, 여기 『원서 읽는 단어장』이 왔습니다!
원서 읽는 단어장은, 영어 원서에 나온 어려운 어휘들을 완벽히 정리해서

원서 읽기의 부담감을 줄이고 보다 효과적으로 영어 실력을 쌓을 수 있도록 도와주는 책입니다. 또한 이해력을 점검하는 Comprehension Quiz를 통해 내가 원서를 정확히 읽고 있는지 확인해볼 수 있습니다.

『원서 읽는 단어장』시리즈를 통해 영어 원서를 보다 쉽고 재미있게 읽고, 영어 실력도 쑥쑥 향상시켜보세요.

이 책은 Roald Dahl(로알드 달)의 대표작 Matilda(마틸다) 독자들을 위해 만들어졌습니다. 위 영어 원서는 시중 서점 및 인터넷 서점에서 쉽게 구입할 수 있습니다.

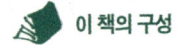 **이 책의 구성**

Comprehension Quiz

원서를 제대로 읽고 이해하고 있는지 측정해보는 간단한 퀴즈입니다.

원어민 Extensive Reading 전문가가 출제한 쉽고 재미있는 문제들로 구성되어 있습니다. 퀴즈를 풀어보고 틀린 부분이 있다면, 제대로 이해한 것이 맞는지 해당 내용을 다시 한 번 점검해봐야겠죠?

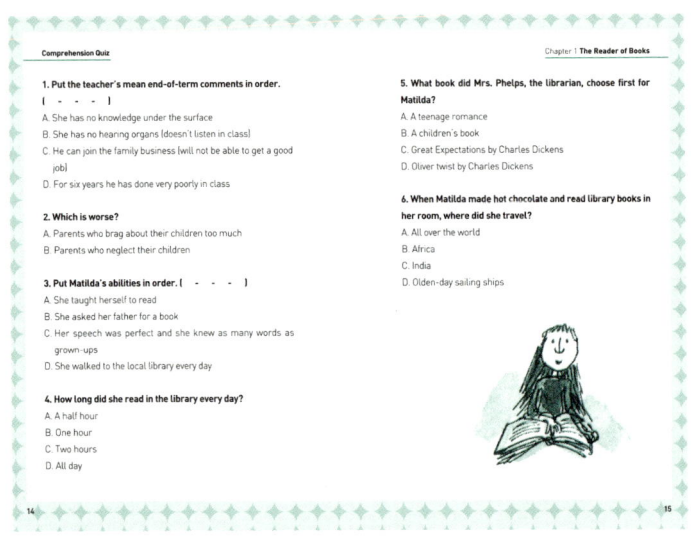

퀴즈는 각 챕터별로 약 5개 안팎의 문제가 출제되어 있습니다.

각 챕터를 읽고 바로 문제를 풀어보는 것도 좋고, 혹은 시간이 되는 대로 쭉 읽은 후 해당 부분만큼 문제를 풀어보는 것도 좋은 방법입니다. 내 상황과 스타일에 맞게 적절히 활용하세요!

정답은 128페이지에 있습니다.

Build your Vocabulary

원서에 등장하는 어려운 어휘가 정리되어 있습니다.

단어는 각 챕터별로, 원서에서 단어가 등장하는 순서 그대로 정리되어 있으며, [빈도-스펠링-발음기호-한글 뜻-영어 뜻] 순으로 표기되어 있습니다.

별표(★)가 많을수록 필수 어휘입니다. 또 이전 챕터에서 등장한 중요 어휘가 반복해서 나올 때는 '복습'이라고 표시해서 정리했습니다.

특히 로알드 달(Roald Dahl)의 대표 세 작품(Charlie and the Chocolate Factory, Matilda, James and the Giant Peach) 단어장에는 빈도 표시와 함께 C(Charlie and the Chocolate Factory에도 나오는 어휘) 또는 J(James and the Giant Peach에도 나오는 어휘) 표시가 되어 있습니다. 이런 단어를 확실히 암기해두면, 이후 시리즈를 읽을 때 큰 도움이 됩니다.

어휘 목록 중에 아주 기초적인 어휘는 제외되어 있습니다. 원서를 읽을 때 여기 나와 있는 단어 외에도 모르는 어휘가 너무 많다면, '내 영어 수준보다 지나치게 어려운 책을 골랐다'는 의미가 됩니다. 이런 경우에는 일단 더 쉬운 원서에 도전하는 것이 좋은 방법입니다.

여기 정리된 단어를 일일이 손으로 쓰면서 '암기'하려고 하지는 마세요! 실질적인 어휘 암기는 원서를 읽으면서 문맥 속에서 단어와 자주 마주칠 때 이루어집니다!

단어 리스트는 원서를 읽기 전, 후에 눈으로 쭉 살피면서 '단어와 익숙해지도록' 만드는 데 활용하세요. 원서를 읽을 때 단어에서 오는 부담감이 줄어들고, 매우 효율적으로 어휘 실력을 향상시킬 수 있습니다.

Crossword Puzzle

잠시 쉬어가면서 낱말 맞추기 퍼즐을 하는 페이지입니다.

각 문제에 해당하는 단어 스펠링을 가로-세로 빈칸에 맞춰서 채워나가면 됩니다.

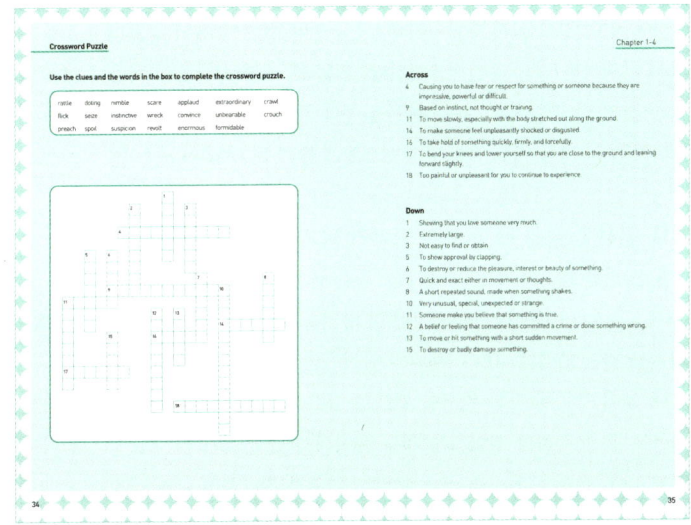

퍼즐의 문제들은 원서에서 반복해서 등장하는 중요 어휘로 구성되어 있습니다. 편안한 마음으로 퍼즐을 풀어보세요! 그러다보면 어휘 실력도 더욱 탄탄하게 다져질 것입니다.

정답은 130 페이지에 있습니다.

영어 원서 읽기 전문가가 대답해주는 FAQ

Q. 원서를 읽고 싶은데 어떤 책으로 시작할지 모르겠어요.

A. 원서를 고를 때는 '나의 영어 수준'과 '나의 관심 분야', 이 두 가지만 생각하면 됩니다. 꼭 읽고 싶은 책이 내 영어 수준에도 적합하다면, 그게 설사 영어로 쓰여 있다 해도 쉽고 재미있게 읽을 수 있습니다. 한글로 감명 깊게 읽었던 책이나 전공·업무에 연관된 책 중에서 수준에 맞는 원서를 찾아보세요. 베스트셀러 소설이나 자기 계발서 중에서 골라 읽는 것도 좋은 방법입니다.

아직 영어 원서 읽기 초보자라면, 관심 분야보다는 '영어 수준'에 초점을 맞춰서 선택하는 것을 추천해드립니다. 또한 내 수준보다 조금 쉬운 원서를 고르는 것이 더 좋습니다. 쉬운 원서를 통해 완독의 기쁨을 맛보고 4~5권 이상 읽다보면 그 다음 읽을 책들이 자연스럽게 눈에 띌 것입니다!

Q. 원서를 읽을 때 모르는 단어가 나오면 어떻게 하죠?

A. 사전을 찾으면서 읽는 경우는 중간에 지쳐 포기할 확률이 높습니다. 따라서 모르는 단어가 나온다고 일일이 사전을 찾으면서 읽지는 마세요. 모르는 어휘는 일단 문맥에 따라 이해하고 넘어가면 됩니다.

내 영어 수준에 맞는 원서를 제대로 골랐다면, 어려운 어휘가 많지도 않고 그 의미를 추측하고 넘어가는 것도 용이해서 별 문제가 되지 않을 것입니다. 반면 너무 어려운 원서를 골라 모르는 어휘가 지나치게 많이 등장한다면, 문맥에 따라 의미를 추측하는 것은 사실상 불가능합니다. 한 페이지(250단어)당 모르는 어휘가 10개가 넘는다면 지나치게 어려운 원서를 골랐다고 볼 수 있습니다. 수준에 맞는 원서를 고르고, 실력 향상에 맞춰 원서 수준도 높여가세요.

사실 어휘력을 쌓는다는 측면에서만 보면, 모르는 단어를 찾아보며 읽는 것도 좋은 방법입니다. 다만, 사전만 들여다보다 지치지 않도록 균형을 맞추는 것이 중요하겠지요. 만약 미리 누군가 어려운 단어를 정리해줬다면, 그보다 더 좋을 수는 없을 것입니다. (그래서 이런 원서 읽는 단어장이 있는 것이겠죠?)

Q. 이 원서가 너무 어렵게 느껴지는데… 계속 읽어야 할까요?

A. 어려워도 꼭 읽고 싶다는 생각이 드는 책이라면 계속 읽는 것이 좋지만, 그렇지 않은 책이라면 과감히 포기하는 것이 좋습니다. 원서 읽기를 통한 영어 공부에서 가장 중요한 것은 '스트레스 받지 않고 즐겁게' 읽는 것입니다. 어려운 원서로 스트레스만 받는다면, 꾸준히 읽지도 못하고 영어 실력도 향상되기 힘듭니다. 더 쉽고 관심 있는 책을 골라보세요.

Q. 제대로 이해하는 건지 걱정이 되는데, 번역서를 같이 보고 읽는 것은 어떤가요?

A. 추천하지 않습니다. 번역 역시 100% 완벽하다고 할 수 없을뿐더러, 영어를 한글로 바꿔야만 직성이 풀리는 좋지 않은 리딩 습관을 기를 수 있기 때문입니다.

번역된 책과 함께 읽기보다, '영화'와 함께 읽는 것을 추천합니다. 즉, 영화화 된 원서 혹은 영화 기반의 원서를 읽는 것이지요. 영화를 보고 해당 원서를 읽으면, 이미 대략적인 내용을 파악한 상태라 보다 수월하게 리딩 할 수 있기 때문입니다. 또 내용에 따른 전후 상황, 느낌과 분위기, 뉘앙스 등을 영화를 통해 파악했기 때문에 리딩 시에 '보다 폭넓은 이해'가 가능합니다.

'글을 읽는다'는 것은 단순히 '무슨 내용인지 안다'는 의미가 아닙니다. 왜 이런 상황에서 이런 이야기를 하는지, 등장인물은 어떤 감정으로 대화하고 있는지, 작가는 글을 통해 어떻게 효과적으로 정보를 전달하는지, 이런 점들까지 폭넓게 바라볼 수 있어야 '글을 제대로 읽는다'고 할 수 있습니다. 영화와 함께 원서를 읽는 것은 이런 깊이 있는 리딩 훈련이 자연스럽게 이루어지도록 도와줍니다.

Comprehension Quiz
Build Your Vocabulary
Crossword Puzzle

Comprehension Quiz

1. Put the teacher's mean end-of-term comments in order.
(- - -)

A. She has no knowledge under the surface

B. She has no hearing organs (doesn't listen in class)

C. He can join the family business (will not be able to get a good job)

D. For six years he has done very poorly in class

2. Which is worse?

A. Parents who brag about their children too much

B. Parents who neglect their children

3. Put Matilda's abilities in order. (- - -)

A. She taught herself to read

B. She asked her father for a book

C. Her speech was perfect and she knew as many words as grown-ups

D. She walked to the local library every day

4. How long did she read in the library every day?

A. A half hour

B. One hour

C. Two hours

D. All day

Chapter 1 **The Reader of Books**

5. What book did Mrs. Phelps, the librarian, choose first for Matilda?

A. A teenage romance

B. A children's book

C. Great Expectations by Charles Dickens

D. Oliver twist by Charles Dickens

6. When Matilda made hot chocolate and read library books in her room, where did she travel?

A. All over the world

B. Africa

C. India

D. Olden-day sailing ships

Comprehension Quiz

1. What did Mr. and Mrs. Wormwood look like?

A. Mr. Wormwood •

B. Mrs. Wormwood •

- a. A dog-faced man with dark striped clothes
- b. A dark haired skinny witch
- c. A platinum blond woman with bulging fat everywhere
- d. A rat-faced man with bright check clothes

2. How did Mr. Wormwood trick customers into buying cars? (two answers)

A. He washed the car

B. He put saw dust in the oil

C. He fixed the gears

D. He wound the speedometer back

3. How many miles did Mr. Wormwood leave on the speedometer?

A. One mile

B. Ten miles

C. One thousand miles

D. Ten thousand miles

Chapter 2 **Mr. Wormwood, the Great Car Dealer**

4. What does Matilda not think of her father's car selling ideas?

A. She thinks the ideas are dishonest

B. She thinks the ideas are disgusting

C. She thinks the ideas are cheating

D. She thinks the ideas should be a secret

5. Why did Matilda decide to get back at her parents? (two answers)

A. Because it would stop her from going crazy

B. Because they told her that she was stupid

C. Because they watched television at dinner

D. Because her parents did not read books

Comprehension Quiz

1. What did Mr. Wormwood's hat look like?

A. A round bowler hat

B. A wide brimmed farmer's hat

C. A flat-topped pork pie hat

D. A fur hat

2. Put the events in order. (- - -)

A. Matilda put superglue around the inside of the hat

B. Matilda used a walking stick to get the hat down

C. Mr. Wormwood put the hat on

D. She hooked the hat back on the peg

3. Why did Mr. Wormwood pretend to want to wear his hat all day at work?

A. Because he wanted to look like a gangster

B. Because he wanted to save face

C. Because he liked it

D. Because he usually did

Chapter 3 **The Hat and the Superglue**

4. What does Mrs. Wormwood not think about the boy who accidentally superglued his finger in his nose?

A. He probably learned to stop picking his nose

B. Picking your nose is a nasty habit

C. I pick my nose too

D. It serves him right for picking his nose

5. Why does Mrs. Wormwood cut her husband's hat off?

A. Because he can't sleep and take shower

B. Because he likes the hat so much

C. Because he can't sell cars

D. Because he can't watch the television

6. What does Matilda think of the hat prank?

A. It is funny but she feels a little bit sorry

B. Her father's forehead looks like it has lice crawling on it

C. Her father has learned an important lesson

D. Her father looks like a monk

Comprehension Quiz

1. Why does Mr. Wormwood tear up the book?

A. Because Matilda ask for him to do it

B. Because he is angry

C. Because the book is deadly boring

D. Because the TV is too loud

2. What can the parrot say? (two answers)

A. Shiver me timbers

B. Hello

C. Polly want a cracker

D. Rattle my bones

Chapter 4 **The Ghost**

3. Where did Matilda put the parrot's cage?

A. She hung it on the ceiling

B. She hided it in the Kitchen

C. She wedged it up the chimney

D. She put it in her room

4. In what order did the family go into the dining-room.

A. ____ Father

B. ____ Mother

C. ____ Brother

D. ____ Matilda

5. When the "ghost" said "rattle my bones" everyone jumped. Why did Matilda jump too?

A. Because she was scared

B. Because she was pretending to be scared

C. Because she saw a real ghost

D. Because she saw a grumpy sooty parrot

Build your Vocabulary

1. The Reader of Books

blister [blístər] *n.* (구어) 싫은 녀석; 물집, 수포; 부풉 *v.* 물집이 생기다
Some lazy bastard who always appears after the hard work has been finished.

adoration [ӕdəréiʃən] *n.* 예배, 숭배, 애모, 동경
Very strong love for someone.

convince [kənvíns] *vt.* 확신시키다, 납득시키다
To make you believe that something is true.

revolt [rivóult] *v.* 비위가 상하다[게 하다]; 반항[배반]하다; *n.* 반란, 폭동
To make someone feel unpleasantly shocked or disgusted.

offspring [ɔ́(:)fspriŋ] *n.* (pl.) 자식, 자녀들; 자손, 후예
A person's children.

basin [béisən] *n.* 물동이, 대야, 세면기
An open round container shaped like a bowl with sloping sides, used for holding food or liquid.

twaddle [twádəl] *n.* 실없는[허튼] 소리; 객설을 농하는 자; *vi.* 실없는 소리를 하다
Speech or writing which is foolish or not true; nonsense.

cook up *idiom* ① …을 재빨리 요리하다 ② …을 조작하다, 지어내다
To invent a story, plan, etc., usually dishonestly.

scorcher [skɔ́:rtʃər] *n.* 통렬한 비난[비평]; 몹시 뜨거운 것; 타는 듯이 더운 날

doting [dóutiŋ] *a.* 지나치게 사랑하는; 망령 든
Showing that you love someone very much.

lyrical [lírikəl] *a.* 서정시조의, 서정미가 있는, 감상적인; 고양된
Expressing personal thoughts and feelings in a beautiful way.

abdomen [ǽbdəmən] *n.* 배, 복부; (곤충 따위의) 복부
The end part of an insect's body that is attached to its thorax.

delve [delv] *v.* (서적·기록 등을) 탐구하다, 깊이 파고들다; 아래로 급경사지다
To search, especially as if by digging, in order to find a thing or information.

cicada [sikéidə] *n.* 매미
A large insect found in warm countries, which produces a high continuous sound.

Chapter 1-4

* **grub** [grʌb] *n.* 굼벵이, 구더기, 유충
An insect in the stage when it has just come out of its egg.

chrysalis [krísəlis] *n.* 번데기, 유충; 미숙한 기간
An insect covered by a hard protective case at the stage of development before it becomes a moth or butterfly with wings, or the case itself.

⁂ **sting** [stiŋ] *v.* 찌르다, 쏘다; 괴롭히다, 고통을 주다; 얼얼하다, 자극하다
To make somebody feel angry or upset.

glacial [gléiʃəl] *a.* 얼음의; 빙하의
Made or left by a glacier.

stinker [stíŋkər] *n.* 불쾌한 놈, 골칫거리
Someone or something that is very unpleasant.

scab [skæb] *n.* 인간쓰레기
A worker who refuses to join a strike or takes the place of somebody on strike.

* **flick** [flik] *n.* (매·채찍 따위로) 찰싹[탁] 때리기; *v.* 찰싹[탁] 치다
To move or hit something with a short sudden movement.

CJ ⁂ **enormous** [inɔ́ːrməs] *a.* 막대한, 거대한
Extremely large.

bunions [bʌ́njən] *n.* [병리] 건막류(腱膜瘤) (엄지발가락 안쪽의 염증)
A painful swelling on the first joint of the big toe.

CJ ⁂ **extraordinary** [ikstrɔ́ːrdənèri] *a.* 대단한, 비상한, 비범한; 터무니없는
Very unusual, special, unexpected or strange.

* **nimble** [nímbəl] *a.* 재빠른, 민첩한; 영리한, 빈틈없는; 재치[재주] 있는
Quick and exact either in movement or thoughts.

half-witted [hǽfwìtid] *a.* 얼빠진; 정신박약의
Stupid.

gormless [gɔ́ːrmlis] *a.* (영·구어) 얼뜬, 아둔한
Stupid and slow to understand.

J ⁂ **crawl** [krɔːl] *vi.* 기어가다, 느릿느릿 가다
To move slowly, especially with the body stretched out along the ground.

Build your Vocabulary

* **applaud** [əplɔ́ːd] v. 박수를 보내다, 성원하다
To show approval by clapping.

hanker [hǽŋkər] vi. 동경하다, 갈망[열망]하다
To have a strong desire for something, especially if you cannot or should not have it.

* **flaming** [fléimiŋ] n. 불타는; 타는 듯이 붉은; 열정에 불타는, 열렬한
A powerful feeling.

telly [téli] n. (영·구어) 텔레비전 (수상기)

c ** **spoil** [spɔil] vt. 망쳐놓다, 손상하다; 버릇없이 기르다
To destroy or reduce the pleasure, interest or beauty of something.

be hooked on idiom (구어) …에 맛들이다, 중독되어 있다; 열중해 있다
If you are hooked into something, or hook into something, you get involved with it.

* **awhile** [əhwáil] ad. 잠깐, 잠시 (for a while)
For a short time.

toddle [tádl] vi. 출발하다; 아장아장 걷다, 거닐다
To walk with short steps, trying to keep the body balanced.

cosy [kóuzi] (=cozy) a. (방 등이) (따뜻하여) 기분 좋은, 편안한; 아늑한
Comfortable and pleasant, especially because small and warm.

** **devour** [diváuər] vt. 게걸스럽게 먹다, 먹어치우다
To eat something eagerly and in large amounts so that nothing is left.

* **fascination** [fæ̀sənéiʃən] n. 매혹, 매료, 황홀케 함, 홀린 상태
The state of being greatly interested in or delighted by something.

* **stun** [stʌn] vt. 어리벙벙하게 하다, 기절시키다
To shock or surprise someone very much.

* **instinctive** [instíŋktiv] a. 본능적인, 직관적인; 무의식적인
Based on instinct, not thought or training.

** **expectation** [èkspektéiʃən] n. 예상, 기대
Strong hopes or beliefs that something will happen.

* **cobweb** [kábwèb] vt. 거미줄로 덮다; n. 거미줄
A net-like structure of sticky silk threads made by a spider for catching insects.

mooch [muːtʃ] *v.i.* 배회하다, 살금살금 거닐다
To walk or act slowly and without much purpose.

astound [əstáund] *v.t.* 깜짝 놀라게 하다, 몹시 놀라게 하다
If something astounds you, you are very surprised by it.

compassionate [kəmpǽʃənit] *a.* 인정 많은, 동정심이 있는, 자비로운
Feeling or showing sympathy for people who are suffering.

formidable [fɔ́ːrmidəbəl] *a.* 무서운; 만만찮은, 얕잡을 수 없는; 굉장히 많은
Causing you to have fear or respect for something or someone because they are impressive, powerful or difficult.

tempt [tempt] *v.t.* 유혹하다, 부추기다
Something that tempts you attracts you and makes you want it.

fuss [fʌs] *n.* 야단법석, 호들갑
Attention and excitement given to small and unimportant matters.

2. Mr Wormwood, the Great Car Dealer

sawdust [sɔ́ːdʌst] *n.* 톱밥
The dust and small pieces of wood which are produced when you cut wood with a saw.

sawmill [sɔ́ːmìl] *n.* 제재소; 제재용 톱
A factory where trees are cut up into pieces with machines.

ignorant [ígnərənt] *a.* 무지한, 예의를 모르는, (어떤 일을) 모르는
Not polite or respectful.

twit [twit] *n.* 바보
A stupid person.

boast [boust] *v.* 자랑하다; *n.* 자랑거리, 허풍
To speak too proudly or happily about what you have done or what you own.

egg [ég] ① *v.t.* 선동하다, 부추기다; ② *n.* 알, 달걀
If you egg a person on, you encourage them to do something, especially something dangerous or foolish.

rattle [rǽtl] *n.* 덜거덕거리는 소리; *v.* 덜거덕거리며 움직이다
A short repeated sound, made when something shakes.

Build your Vocabulary

diddle [dídl] *vt.* (구어) 속이다, 속여서 빼앗다
To obtain money from someone in a way which is not honest.

c **moustache** [mʎstæʃ] (=mustache) *n.* (미) 코밑수염, 동물의 수염
Hair which a man grows above his upper lip.

speedometer [spi:dámitər] *n.* (자동차 등의) 속도계; 주행 기록계
A device in a vehicle which shows how fast the vehicle is moving.

J * **fiddle** [fídl] *v.* 바이올린을 켜다; 시간을 보내다; (사람·숫자 등을) 속이다
To change the details or figures of something in order to try to get money dishonestly, or gain an advantage.

* **ruddy** [rʎdi] *a.* 붉은, 불그스름한; (영·속어) 싫은, 괘씸한
To be used to avoid saying bloody to express anger or annoyance.

‡ **temper** [témpər] *v.* 완화하다, 부드럽게 하다; 조화시키다; *n.* 기질, 기분
To make something less severe by adding something that has the opposite effect.

‡ **inherit** [inhérit] *v.* 상속하다, 물려받다, 유전하다
To receive money, a house, etc. from someone after they have died.

crookery [kruks] *n.* 도둑 기질
Dishonest.

penicillin [pènəsílin] *n.* [약학] 페니실린
A type of medicine which kills bacteria; a type of antibiotic.

Eureka [juərí:kə] *int.* (익살) 알았다, 됐다 (아르키메데스가 왕관의 금(金) 순도 측정법을 발견했을 때 지른 소리)
Used to show that you have been successful in something you were trying to do.

CJ ‡ **tremendous** [triméndəs] *a.* 거대한, 대단한; 엄청난, 무서운
Very great in amount or level, or extremely good.

‡ **jug** [dʒʌg] *n.* (속어) 교도소, 감옥
Prison.

* **mint** [mint] *n.* (금전 따위의) 거액, 막대한 양
(a mint) A large amount of money.

* **archbishop** [à:rtʃbíʃəp] *n.* [가톨릭·그리스정교·영국국교] 대주교
A bishop of the highest rank, responsible for all the churches in a large area.

★ **Canterbury** [kǽntərbèri] *n.* 캔터베리 (영국 켄트 주의 도시)

‡ **preach** [pri:tʃ] *v.* 설교하다, 전도하다
To give a religious speech.

C **squirt** [skwə:rt] *n.* (구어) 건방진 벼락부재[젊은이]; 꼬마; *v.* 분출시키다, 뿜다
A young or small person whom you consider to be unimportant and who has behaved rudely towards you.

CJ ‡ **nasty** [nǽsti] *a.* 더러운, 불쾌한, 몹시 싫은; 심술궂은, 험악한
Bad or very unpleasant.

C ★ **munch** [mʌntʃ] *v.* 우적우적 먹다
To eat something, especially noisily.

soap-opera *n.* (미) 연속 홈[멜로] 드라마
A series of television or radio programmes about the lives and problems of a particular group of characters. The series continues over a long period and is broadcast (several times) every week.

‡ **dye** [dai] *v.* 물들이다, 염색하다
To change the colour of something using a special liquid.

CJ ‡ **bulge** [bʌldʒ] *v.* 부풀다, 불룩해지다, 튀어나오다, 부풀리다
To stick out in a round shape.

‡ **flesh** [fleʃ] *n.* 살, 육체
The soft part of the body of a person or animal which is between the skin and the bones.

C ‡ **strap** [stræp] *n.* 가죽 끈, 혁대; *v.* 끈으로 매다, 가죽 끈으로 때리다
To fasten something in position by fixing a narrow piece of leather or other strong material around it.

★ **resent** [rizént] *v.* 분개하다
If you resent someone or something, you feel bitter or angry about them, especially because you feel it is unfair.

get one's own back *idiom* (영·구어) …에게 복수하다, 보복하다

C ★ **beastly** [bí:stli] *a.* 짐승 같은; 잔인한; 더러운, 불결한; *ad.* 몹시, 아주
Unkind or unpleasant.

Build your Vocabulary

tolerate [tálərèit] *vt.* 관대히 다루다, 묵인하다; 참다, 견디다
If you tolerate a situation or person, you accept them although you do not particularly like them.

idiocy [ídiəsi] *n.* 백치, 백치 행위
A stupid action, or stupidity.

3. The Hat and the Superglue

cloakroom *n.* (호텔·극장 등의) 코트[휴대품] 보관소
A room in a public building such as a restaurant, theater, etc. where coats, bags, and other personal items can be left while their owners are in the building.

peg [peg] *n.* 나무 못, 쐐기, 걸이 못
A small stick or hook which sticks out from a surface and from which objects, especially clothes, can hang.

rakish [réikiʃ] *a.* 멋진, 날씬한(smart), 쾌활한; (배기) 경쾌한
A rakish person or appearance is stylish in a confident, bold way.

rim [rim] *n.* (둥근 물건의) 가장자리, 테두리, 테; *v.* 둘러싸다, 테를 두르다
The outer, often curved or circular, edge of something.

scalp [skælp] *n.* 두피, 머리가죽; *v.* 머리가죽을 벗기다
The skin on the top of a person's head where hair usually grows.

fiddle [fídl] *v.* 바이올린을 켜다; 시간을 보내다; (사람·숫자 등을) 속이다
To change the details or figures of something in order to try to get money dishonestly, or gain an advantage.

yank [jæŋk] *v.* (구어) 확 잡아당기다
To pull something forcefully with a quick movement.

rattle [rǽtl] *n.* 덜거덕거리는 소리; *v.* 덜거덕거리며 움직이다
A short repeated sound, made when something shakes.

nestle [nésəl] *vi.* 편안하게 드러눕다, 기분 좋게 자리 잡다
To rest yourself or part of your body in a warm, comfortable and protected position.

swollen [swóulən] *a.* 부어오른, 부푼; 과장한, 과대한
Larger than usual.

Chapter 1-4

- **suspicion** [səspíʃən] *n.* 혐의, 용의, 의심
  A belief or feeling that someone has committed a crime or done something wrong.

- **nasty** [nǽsti] *a.* 더러운, 불쾌한, 몹시 싫은; 심술궂은, 혐악한
  Bad or very unpleasant.

- **clutch** [klʌtʃ] *vt.* 꽉 잡다, 붙들다
  To take or try to take hold of something tightly.

- **brim** [brim] *n.* 가장자리; 테두리; (모자의) 챙; *v.* 가득 붓다; 넘치다
  The flat edge around the bottom of a hat that sticks out.

- **splutter** [splʌ́tər] (=sputter) *vi.* 푸푸 소리를 내다; 입에서 침을 튀기다
  To speak in a quick and confused way, producing short unclear noises because of surprise, anger, etc., or (of a person or thing) to make a series of noises similar to this.

- **budge** [bʌdʒ] *v.* 움직이기 시작하다; 태도[견해]를 바꾸다
  If someone will not budge on a matter they refuse to change their mind.

- **skulk** [skʌlk] *vi.* 슬그머니 숨다, 잠복하다; 살금살금…하다
  To hide or move around as if trying not to be seen, usually with bad intentions.

- **chop** [tʃap] *v.* 자르다, 잘게 썰다
  To cut something into pieces with an axe, knife or other sharp instrument.

- **monk** [mʌŋk] *n.* 수도사
  A member of a group of religious men who do not marry and usually live together.

- **patch** [pætʃ] *n.* 단편, 파편; 헝겊 조각; *v.* 헝겊을 대고 깁다; 주워 맞추다
  A small piece of material fixed over something to cover it.

- **crawl** [krɔːl] *vi.* 기어가다, 느릿느릿 가다
  To move slowly, especially with the body stretched out along the ground.

- **snap** [snæp] *v.* 날카롭게[느닷없이] 말하다; 홱 잡다, 탁 소리 내다, 덥석 물다
  To say something suddenly in an angry way.

4. The Ghost

- **chasten** [tʃéisən] *vt.* 징벌하다, 억제하다, 누그러지게 하다
  To make somebody feel sorry for something they have done.

Build your Vocabulary

crummy [krʌ́mi] *a.* (속어) 지저분한; 하찮은, 싸구려의
Of very bad quality.

★ **bully** [búli] *vt.* (약한 자를) 들볶다, 위협하다
To hurt or frighten someone who is smaller or less powerful than you, often forcing them to do something they do not want to do.

★ **irritable** [írətəbəl] *a.* 성미가 급한
Becoming annoyed very easily.

simmer down *phrasal v.* 서서히 식다; (노여움 따위가) 가라앉다, 진정되다
To become less angry or excited about something.

‡ **scarce** [skɛərs] *a.* 부족한, 적은, 모자라는; 드문, 희귀한
Not easy to find or obtain.

‡ **stride** [straid] (strode–stridden) *v.* 큰 걸음으로 걷다; *n.* 큰 걸음, 활보
If you stride somewhere, you walk there with quick, long steps.

curl up *idiom* 몸을 둥글게 웅크리다
To sit or lie in a position with your arms and legs close to your body.

blare [blɛər] *v.* 울려 퍼지다, 크게 울리다
To make an unpleasantly loud noise.

CJ ★ **ghastly** [gǽstli] *a.* 핼쑥한, 송장 같은, 무서운
Unpleasant and shocking.

J **infuriate** [infjúərièit] *vt.* 격노케 하다
To make someone extremely angry.

★ **intensify** [inténsəfài] *v.* 강렬하게 하다, 격렬하게 하다, 증강하다
To become greater, more serious or more extreme, or to make something do this.

C ‡ **snatch** [snætʃ] *v.* 와락 붙잡다, 잡아채다
To seize or grab suddenly.

★ **filth** [filθ] *n.* 오물, 불결한 물건, 쓰레기, 더러움
Thick, unpleasant dirt.

★ **rip** [rip] *vt.* 쪼개다, 째다, 찢다
To pull apart; to tear or be torn violently and quickly.

Chapter 1-4

how dare *idiom* 감히 …하다니
You say 'how dare you' when you are very shocked and angry about something that someone has done.

sulk [sʌlk] *n.* 샐쭉함, 부루퉁함; *v.* 샐쭉해지다, 부루퉁해지다, 골나다
To be silent and childishly refuse to smile or be pleasant to people because you are angry about something that they have done.

‡ subtle [sʌtl] *a.* 미묘한, 포착하기 힘든, 희미한
Not loud, bright, noticeable or obvious in any way.

‡ hatch [hætʃ] *v.* (알을) 부화하다; (음모 · 계획을) 꾸미다
To produce (young) from an egg.

‡ investigate [invéstəgèit] *v.* 조사하다, 연구하다, 심사하다
To examine a crime, problem, statement, etc. carefully, especially to discover the truth.

rattle [rǽtl] *n.* 덜거덕거리는 소리; *v.* 덜거덕거리며 움직이다
A short repeated sound, made when something shakes.

spooky [spúːki] *a.* 유령[이 나올 것] 같은; 으스스한, 무시무시한
Strange and frightening.

c **‡ marvellous** [máːrvələs] (=marvelous) *a.* 놀라운, 믿기 어려운
Extremely good.

cJ **★ fabulous** [fǽbjələs] *a.* 굉장한, 멋진; 황당무계한, 믿어지지 않는, 전설적인
Very good; excellent.

c **‡ stagger** [stǽgər] *v.* 비틀거리다[게 하다]; 흔들리다[게 하다]
To walk or move with a lack of balance as if you are going to fall.

c **★ wedge** [wedʒ] *v.* 밀어 넣다, 끼워 넣다; *n.* 쐐기
To force something firmly into a narrow space.

‡ chimney [tʃímni] *n.* 굴뚝
A hollow structure that allows the smoke from a fire inside a building to escape to the air outside.

★ soot [sut] *n.* 검댕, 매연; *v.* 검댕으로 더럽히다, 검댕투성이로 하다
A black powder made mainly of carbon which is produced when coal, wood, etc. is burnt.

Build your Vocabulary

burglar [bə́:rglər] *n.* (주거 침입) 강도, 빈집털이, 밤도둑, (미·속어) 사기꾼
A person who illegally enters buildings and steals things.

hiss [his] *n.* 쉿 소리; *v.* 쉿 하는 소리를 내다
To make a long noise like the letter 's'

collar [kάlər] *vt.* (구어) 체포하다, 붙잡다; 깃을 달다; *n.* 칼라, 깃
To catch and hold someone so that they cannot escape.

dash off *idiom* 급히 떠나다, 돌진하다
If you dash off to a place, you go there very quickly.

wipe [waip] *v.* 훔치다, 닦다, 비비다
To pass over, or rub on to.

poker [póukər] *n.* 부지깽이
A long thin metal stick that you use to move around coal or wood in a fire so that it burns better.

seize [si:z] *vt.* 붙잡다
If you seize something, you take hold of it quickly, firmly, and forcefully.

rip [rip] *vt.* 쪼개다, 째다, 찢다
To pull apart; to tear or be torn violently and quickly.

socket [sάkit] *n.* 꽂는[끼우는] 구멍; (전구 등을 꽂는) 소켓
The part of a piece of equipment, especially electrical equipment, into which another part fits.

creep [kri:p] (crept-crept) *vi.* 기다, 살금살금 걷다
To move slowly, quietly and carefully, usually in order to avoid being noticed.

brandish [brǽndiʃ] *vt.* (검·곤봉·채찍 등을) 휘두르다
To wave something in the air in a threatening or excited way.

shriek [ʃri:k] *n.* 날카로운 소리, 비명; *v.* 새된 소리로 말하다
A short, loud, high cry.

quake [kwéiki] *v.* 덜덜 떨다, 전율하다; 흔들리다, 진동하다
To shake because you are very frightened or nervous.

distinctly [distíŋktli] *a.* 뚜렷한, 명백한; 틀림없는; 별개의, 다른, 독특한
Clearly noticeable; that certainly exists.

Chapter 1-4

clutch [klʌtʃ] *vt.* 꽉 잡다, 붙들다
To take or try to take hold of something tightly.

throttle [θrátl] *vt.* …의 목을 조르다, 질식시키다, 누르다, 억압하다
To press someone's throat very tightly so that they cannot breathe.

flee [fli:] (fled-fled) *vi.* 달아나다, 도망하다, 내빼다
To escape by running away, especially because of danger or fear.

slam [slæm] *vt.* (문 따위를) 탕 닫다, 세게 치다
If you slam something down, you put it there quickly and with great force.

sooty [súti] *a.* 그을린; 검어진, 거무스름한
Something that is sooty is covered with soot.

grumpy [grʌ́mpi] *a.* 까다로운, 기분이 언짢은 (grumpily *ad.* 까다롭게, 언짢게)
Easily annoyed and complaining.

Crossword Puzzle

Use the clues and the words in the box to complete the crossword puzzle.

rattle doting nimble scarce applaud extraordinary crawl
flick seize instinctive wreck convince unbearable formidable
crouch spoil suspicion revolt enormous

Chapter 1-4

Across

4. Causing you to have fear or respect for something or someone because they are impressive, powerful or difficult.
9. Based on instinct, not thought or training.
11. To move slowly, especially with the body stretched out along the ground.
14. To make someone feel unpleasantly shocked or disgusted.
16. To take hold of something quickly, firmly, and forcefully.
17. To bend your knees and lower yourself so that you are close to the ground and leaning forward slightly.
18. Too painful or unpleasant for you to continue to experience.

Down

1. Showing that you love someone very much.
2. Extremely large.
3. Not easy to find or obtain.
5. To show approval by clapping.
6. To destroy or reduce the pleasure, interest or beauty of something.
7. Quick and exact either in movement or thoughts.
8. A short repeated sound, made when something shakes.
10. Very unusual, special, unexpected or strange.
11. Someone make you believe that something is true.
12. A belief or feeling that someone has committed a crime or done something wrong.
13. To move or hit something with a short sudden movement.
15. To destroy or badly damage something.

Comprehension Quiz

1. How much money did Mr. Wormwood make today?

A. 430 pounds & 50 pence

B. 4033 ponds & 15pence

C. 4303 pounds & 50 pence

D. 4330 pounds & 50 pence

2. What did Mr. Wormwood think when he saw that Matilda was right? (two answers)

A. Matilda is a genius

B. Matilda is a cheat

C. Matilda is good at math

D. Matilda looked on his paper from across the room

3. What did Mrs. Wormwood bring home for dinner?

A. Sandwiches

B. Steak

C. Fish and Chips

D. Noodles

Chapter 5 **Arithmetic**

4. Why doesn't Mrs. Wormwood cook dinner?

A. She is too tired from playing bingo

B. She does not like to cook

C. She does not know how to cook

D. She cooks for other people

Comprehension Quiz

1. What did Mr. Wormwood put in his hair every morning?

A. Hair dye

B. A smelly purple bottle

C. Soap

D. Oil of Violets Hair Tonic

2. What does Mr. Wormwood not eat for breakfast?

A. Fried tomatoes

B. Peanut butter and jam

C. Sausage and bacon

D. Fried Eggs

3. Why does Mr. Wormwood always make noise before entering a room? (two answers)

A. He wants to be respected

B. He wants to be noticed

C. He wants to be noisy

D. He wants to make a lot of money

4. Why didn't Matilda dare to look up?

A. She did not want to talk to her father

B. She was not sure she could keep a straight face

C. She was very hungry

D. She was very sad

Chapter 6 **The Platinum-Blond Man**

5. What was Matilda's explanation for her father's hair dye mix up?

A. You wanted to dye your hair

B. You must have taken mummy's bottle of hair stuff off of the shelf instead of your own

C. You must have put your head in the lavatory

D. You must have disinfected your head

Comprehension Quiz

1. Which does not describe Miss Honey?

A. She has light brown hair

B. She is slim and fragile

C. She has a dark v-shaped face

D. She is twenty-three

2. Which does not describe Miss Trunchbull?

A. She is a gigantic tyrannical monster

B. She frightens the life out of teachers and students alike

C. She snorts as she marches down the hall

D. She crushes children under her feet like a tank

3. What does Miss Honey tell the students about Miss Trunchbull?

A. Never murmur something

B. Never answer back

C. Always be looked full of energy

D. She can squash you like a hammer on a grape

4. Why doesn't Matilda want to recite her limerick?

A. Because it is not good

B. Because it has the teacher's first name in it

C. Because it is hard to make one

D. Because the other children will hate her

Chapter 7 **Miss Honey**

5. Why does Miss Honey think that Matilda is a genius?
[two answers]

A. Because Matilda is kind

B. Because Matilda can multiply anything

C. Because she has read Lewis, Tolkien, and Dickens

D. Because Matilda thinks books should have funny bits in them

Comprehension Quiz

1. What is not the qualities of most head teachers?

A. They understand children

B. They are fair and deeply interested in education

C. They are absentminded

D. They have the children's best interests at heart

2. Which is not a feature of Miss Trunchbull's face?

A. A hairy moustache

B. An obstinate chin

C. A cruel mouth

D. Small arrogant eyes

Chapter 8 **The Trunchbull**

3. Why does Miss Trunchbull hate Matilda already? (two answers)

A. Mr. Wormwood said that Matilda was a bad lot

B. Miss Trunchbull thinks that Matilda is a genius

C. Miss Trunchbull thinks that Matilda is very pretty and smart

D. Miss Trunchbull doesn't like any children

4. What happened to Miss Trunchbull when she heard that Matilda was a genius?

A. Her face turned purple

B. Her body swelled up like a bullfrog

C. She said What piffle is this you must be out of your mind

D. She exploded

5. Match the statements and Miss Trunchbull's responses.

Miss Honey	Trunchbull
A. She can multiply	1. So can I
B. She can read	2. She is a parrot
C. She should be moved	3. You're darn right it is up to me to the top form
D. It is up to you, Headmistress	4. So you can't handle her

Build your Vocabulary

5. Arithmetic

arithmetic [ərίθmətik] *n.* 산수, 셈
The part of mathematics that involves the adding and multiplying, etc. of numbers.

long [lɔːŋ] *vi.* 간절히 바라다, 동경하다; *a.* 긴, 오랜
To want something very much.

honourable [ánərəbəl] (=honorable) *a.* 명예로운, 영광스러운; 존경할 만한
Honest and fair, or deserving praise and respect.

put up with *idiom* …을 참고 견디다, 참다
If you put up with something, you tolerate or accept it, even though you find it unpleasant or unsatisfactory.

bearable [bɛ́ərəbəl] *a.* 견딜 수 있는, (추위·더위 등이) 견딜 만한
If an unpleasant situation is bearable, you can accept or deal with it.

sheer [ʃiər] *a.* 얇은, 순전한, 섞이지 않은; 깎아지는 듯한; *ad.* 완전히, 순전히
Used to emphasize how very great, important or powerful a quality or feeling is; nothing except.

run rings around *idiom* (구어) …보다 훨씬 빨리 가다, 훨씬 낫다, 능가하다
If someone runs rings round you, they are very much better, faster, or more successful at something than you are.

oblige [əbláidʒ] *vt.* 강요하다, 은혜를 베풀다
To force someone to do something, or to make it necessary for someone to do something.

asinine [ǽsənàin] *a.* 나귀(ass)의, 나귀 같은; 우둔한(stupid), 고집이 센, 완고한
Extremely stupid.

dread [dred] *a.* 대단히 무서운; *v.* 두려워하다; *n.* 공포
Terrible and greatly feared.

safety-valve (감정·정력 등의) 배출구; (보일러의) 안전판
A way of getting rid of strong feelings without causing harm.

go (a)round the bend *idiom* 미치다; 방향 전환하다; 모퉁이를 돌다

dish out *idiom* (구어) …을 분배하다, 아낌없이 제공하다; (요리)를 덜어주다
If someone dishes out criticism or punishment, they give it to someone.

Chapter 5-8

cocky [káki] *a.* (구어) 잘난 체하는; 건방진
Too confident about yourself in a way that annoys other people.

＊unbearable [ʌnbɛ́ərəbəl] *a.* 견딜 수 없는, 참을 수 없는
Too painful or unpleasant for you to continue to experience.

C ＊**dose** [dous] *n.* (약의) 1회분, 복용량; (쓴) 약; 약간의 경험
A measured amount of something such as medicine.

‡ **alas** [əlǽs] *int.* 아아, 슬프도다!, 불쌍한지고!
Used to express sadness or regret.

flare-up *n.* 번쩍 빛남, 섬광; (구어) (감정의) 격발, 불끈 화를 냄
If there is a flare-up of violence or of an illness, it suddenly starts or gets worse.

＊**appall** [əpɔ́:l] *vt.* 오싹 소름이 끼치게 하다, 섬뜩하게 하다
To make someone have strong feelings of shock or of disapproval.

onlooker [ánlùkər] *n.* 방관자, 구경꾼
Someone who watches something that is happening in a public place but is not involved in it.

복습 **sawdust** [sɔ́:dʌ̀st] *n.* 톱밥
The dust and small pieces of wood which are produced when you cut wood with a saw.

obedient [oubí:diənt] *a.* 순종하는, 고분고분한
Doing, or willing to do, what you have been told to do by someone in authority.

nifty [nifti] *a.* (구어) 익살맞은, 재치 있는, 멋들어진
Good, pleasing or effective.

복습 **diddle** [didl] *vt.* (구어) 속이다, 속여서 빼앗다
To obtain money from someone in a way which is not honest.

J ‡ **wreck** [rek] *v.* 파괴하다, 부수다, 난파시키다; *n.* 난파, 파선, 조난
To destroy or badly damage something.

CJ ＊**crouch** [krautʃ] *v.* 몸을 구부리다, 쭈그리다, 웅크리다
To bend your knees and lower yourself so that you are close to the ground and leaning forward slightly.

hot stuff *n.* (속어) (능력 · 품질 등이) 뛰어난 사람[것]; 유행하는 것; 밀매품
A person who is very skilful at something.

Build your Vocabulary

C **goggle** [gágəl] *v.* (눈알이) 희번덕거리다; 눈알을 굴리다
To look with the eyes wide open because you are surprised.

butt in *idiom* (구어) …에 참견하다, 주제넘게 나서다
If you say that someone is butting in, you are criticizing the fact that they are joining in a conversation or activity without being asked to.

‡ **rubbish** [rʌ́biʃ] *n.* 쓰레기, 폐물; 어리석은 짓
Waste material or unwanted or worthless things.

‡ **exhaust** [igzɔ́:st] *vt.* 다 써버리다, 지치게 하다; *n.* 배출, 배기
To use something completely.

6. The Platinum-Blond Man

foulness [fáulnis] *n.* 부정, 악랄; 불결, 입이 상스러움; (날씨의) 사나움
Dirtiness, unpleasantness, coarseness.

‡ **dye** [dai] *v.* 물들이다, 염색하다
To change the colour of something using a special liquid.

tightrope [táitròup] *n.* (줄타기하는) 팽팽한 줄; (비유) 위험이 내포된 상황
(a tightrope-walker : 줄타기 곡예사)
You can use tightrope in expressions such as walk a tightrope and live on a tightrope to indicate that someone is in a difficult situation and has to be very careful about what they say or do.

freshen [fréʃən] *v.* 신선하게 하다, 새롭게 하다; 새로이 힘을 북돋우다
If the wind freshens, it becomes stronger and colder.

CJ 복습 **nasty** [nǽsti] *a.* 더러운, 불쾌한, 몹시 싫은; 심술궂은, 험악한
Bad or very unpleasant.

peroxide [pəráksaid] *n.* 과산화수소수
A liquid chemical used to make hair very pale in colour or to kill bacteria.

복습 **fascination** [fæ̀sənéiʃən] *n.* 매혹, 매료, 황홀케 함, 홀린 상태
The state of being greatly interested in or delighted by something.

C ‡ **crop** [krɑp] *n.* 수확, 농작물, 곡물
A plant such as a grain, fruit or vegetable grown in large amounts.

Chapter 5-8

- **exceedingly** [iksí:diŋli] *ad.* 대단히, 매우, 몹시
  To a very great degree; extremely.

- **vigorous** [vígərəs] *a.* 원기 왕성한, 활발한
  Very forceful or energetic.

- **masculine** [mǽskjəlin] *a.* 남성의, 남자의, 남자다운, 힘센; *n.* 남자, 남성
  Having characteristics that are traditionally thought to be typical of or suitable for men.

- **grunt** [grʌnt] *v.* (돼지가) 꿀꿀거리다, 툴툴거리다
  To make a short low sound instead of speaking, usually because of anger or pain.

- **tip** [tip] *v.* 기울이다, 뒤집어엎다
  To move so that one side is higher than another side.

- **drain** [drein] *n.* 배수관, 하수구; *v.* 배수[배출]하다; 다 써버리다
  If you drain something, you remove the liquid from it, usually by pouring it away or allowing it to flow away, and if something drains, liquid flows away or out of it.

- **devour** [diváuər] *v.* 게걸스럽게 먹다, 먹어치우다
  To eat something eagerly and in large amounts so that nothing is left.

- **hunk** [hʌŋk] *n.* 두꺼운 조각, 큰 덩어리
  A large thick piece, especially of food.

- **smother** [smʌ́ðər] *v.* 숨막히게 하다, 질식시키다; *n.* 연기 나는 것, 혼란
  To kill someone by covering their face so that they cannot breathe.

- **incapable** [inkéipəbəl] *a.* 할 수 없는, 불가능한; 부적격한; 무능한, 무력한
  Unable to do something.

- **clatter** [klǽtər] *n.* 덜컥덜컥하는 소리; *v.* 달가닥달가닥 울리다
  To make continuous loud noises by hitting hard objects against each other, or to cause objects to do this.

- **flog** [flɑg] *v.* 매질하다, 채찍질하다
  To beat someone very hard with a whip or a stick, as a punishment.

- **dare** [dɛər] *v.* 감히 ···하다, 무릅쓰다, 도전하다
  To be brave enough to do something difficult or dangerous.

- **shriek** [ʃri:k] *n.* 날카로운 소리, 비명; *v.* 새된 소리로 말하다
  A short, loud, high cry.

Build your Vocabulary

- **quiver** [kwívər] *vi.* 떨리다, 흔들리다
  To shake slightly, often because of strong emotion

- **for heaven's sake** *idiom* 제발, 아무쪼록, 부디 (뒤에 오는 명령문을 강조함)
  Used in order to express annoyance or impatience, or to add force to a question or request.

  Oh, My gawd Oh, My God 과 같은 의미로 쓰임

- **splendid** [spléndid] *a.* 화려한, 멋진
  Excellent, or beautiful and impressive.

- **horrendous** [hɔːréndəs] *a.* 무서운, 끔찍한, 무시무시한
  Extremely unpleasant or bad.

- **freak** [friːk] *n.* 이상 현상, 기형, 변덕; 마약 상용자[중독자]; *a.* 진기한, 별난
  A thing, person, animal or event that is extremely unusual or unlikely and not like any other of its type.

- **blaze** [bleiz] *vi.* 타오르다, 빛나다
  To burn brightly and strongly.

- **tweed** [twiːd] *n.* 트위드 (스카치 나사(羅紗)의 일종), (pl.) 트위드 옷
  A thick material woven from wool of several different colours.

- **neat** [niːt] *a.* 산뜻한, 깔끔한 (neatly *ad.* 깔끔하게)
  Tidy, with everything in its place.

- **disinfect** [dìsinfékt] *vt.* 소독하다, 살균하다
  To clean something using chemicals that kill bacteria and other very small living things that cause disease.

- **dilute** [dilúːt] *v.* 묽게 하다, 물을 타다; …의 힘을 약하게 하다; *a.* 묽게 한, 묽은
  To make a liquid weaker by mixing in something else.

- **twit** [twit] *n.* 바보 A stupid person.

- **wail** [weil] *v.* 울부짖다, 통곡하다; *n.* 비탄, 한탄, 울부짖음
  To make a long loud high cry because you are sad or in pain

- **parlour** [páːrlər] *n.* 응접실, 거실; (미) 영업실 (a beauty parlour : 미용실)
  Parlour is used in the names of some types of shops which provide a service, rather than selling things.

7. Miss Honey

- **bleak** [bli:k] *a.* 황폐한, 삭막한, 쓸쓸한
  Cold, empty, and unattractive.

- **oval** [óuvəl] *n.* 타원체; *a.* 타원형의, 달걀 모양의
  A shape like a circle, but wider in one direction than the other.

- **madonna** [mədánə] *n.* (보통 the-) 성모 마리아; 마리아 상(像)
  Mary, the mother of Jesus Christ.

- **fragile** [frǽdʒəl] *a.* 부서지기[깨지기] 쉬운
  Easily damaged, broken or harmed.

- **porcelain** [pɔ́:rsəlin] *a.* 자기로 만든, 깨지기 쉬운; *n.* 자기, (pl.) 자기 제품
  A hard but delicate shiny white substance made by heating a special type of clay to a high temperature, used to make cups, plates, decorations, etc.

- **possess** [pəzés] *v.* 소유하다, 가지고 있다
  To have or own something, or to have a particular quality.

- **adore** [ədɔ́:r] *v.* 숭배하다, 동경하다, 찬미하다; …을 매우 좋아하다
  To love someone very much, especially in an admiring or respectful way, or to like something very much.

- **bewilderment** [biwíldərmənt] *n.* 당황, 어리둥절함
  Bewilderment is the feeling of being bewildered.

- **tangible** [tǽndʒəbəl] *a.* 만져서 알 수 있는, 실체적인; 확실한, 명백한; 현실의
  Real or not imaginary; able to be shown, touched or experienced.

- **gigantic** [dʒaigǽntik] *a.* 거대한, 막대한
  Extremely big.

- **holy** [hóuli] *a.* 신성한
  Related to a religion or a god.

- **tyrannical** [tirǽnikəl] *a.* 폭군의, 폭군 같은; 압제적인, 전제적인, 포악한
  If you describe a government or organization as tyrannical, you mean that it acts without considering the wishes of its people and treats them cruelly or unfairly.

- **menace** [ménəs] *n.* (구어) 골칫거리, 말썽꾸러기; 협박, 공갈
  Something or someone that is very annoying or troublesome.

Build your Vocabulary

come up close *idiom* 가까이 오다

red-hot rod 빨갛게 달궈진 쇠막대기

aswinging 팔을 '좌우로 흔드는' 모습을 묘사한 것

plough [plau] (=plow) *v.* 가르며 나아가다; (쟁기·괭이로) 갈다, 갈아 일구다
When someone ploughs an area of land, they turn over the soil using a plough.

enrage [enréidʒ] *vt.* 노하게 하다
To cause someone to become very angry.

rhinoceros [rainásərəs] *n.* 코뿔소, 무소
A very large thick-skinned animal from Africa or Asia, which has one or two horns on its nose.

eccentricity [èksentrísəti] *n.* (복장·행동 등의) 남다름, 별남; 기행
Eccentricity is unusual behaviour that other people consider strange.

chant [tʃænt] *v.* 일제히 외치다; (노래를) 부르다
To repeat or sing a religious prayer or song to a simple tune.

liquidise [líkwidàiz] (=liquidize) *vt.* 액화하다
To change food into a thick liquid using a blender.

blender [bléndər] *n.* 혼합하는 것[사람]; (미) (부엌용) 믹서
An electric machine for mixing soft food or liquid.

chirrup [tʃírəp] *v.* 지저귀다
To make a short high sound or sounds.

multiplication [mʌ̀ltəplikéiʃən] *n.* 증가; [수학] 곱셈
The act or process of multiplying.

spellbound [spélbàund] *a.* 마법에 걸린, 넋을 잃은
Extremely interested in something.

facility [fəsíləti] *n.* 쉬움, 평이함; 솜씨, (pl.) 편의(를 도모하는 것)
An ability, feature or quality.

solemn [sáləm] *a.* 엄숙한, 근엄한
Serious and without any amusement.

Chapter 5-8

- **polish** [páliʃ] *v.* 윤을 내다, 닦다, 다듬다
  To make something seem better or more attractive.

- **quiver** [kwívər] *vi.* 떨리다, 흔들리다 (quivery *a.* 흔들리는, 떨리는)
  To sound shaky, especially because of emotion.

★ **prodigy** [prádədʒi] *n.* 천재, 신동; 절세의 미인
  Someone with a very great ability which usually shows itself when that person is a young child.

★ **flit** [flit] *vi.* 훌쩍 날다; 휙 지나가다, 오가다
  To fly or move quickly and lightly.

- **purposely** [pə́ːrpəsli] *ad.* 고의로, 일부러
  Intentionally.

C ★ **precious** [préʃəs] *a.* 귀중한, 가치가 있는, 비싼
  Of great value because of being rare, expensive or important.

- **epicure** [épikjùər] *n.* 미식가, 식도락가; (고어) 쾌락주의자
  A person who enjoys food and drink of a high quality; a gourmet.

J ★ **dainty** [déinti] *a.* 섬약한, 섬세한; 까다로운; 맛 좋은, (음식을) 가리는; *n.* 진미
  If you describe a movement, person, or object as dainty, you mean that they are small, delicate, and pretty.

- **limerick** [límərik] *n.* 리머릭 (예전에 아일랜드에서 유행된 5행 행시)
  A humorous poem with five lines.

★ **startle** [stáːrtl] *v.* 깜짝 놀라다
  If something startles you, it surprises and frightens you slightly.

★ **reluctantly** [rilʌ́ktəntli] *ad.* 마지못해, 싫어하면서
  Not very willing to do something and therefore slow to do it.

CJ ★ **scarlet** [skáːrlit] *n.* 주홍색, 진홍색; *a.* 주홍[진홍]색의
  Bright red.

복습 **astound** [əstáund] *vt.* 깜짝 놀라게 하다, 몹시 놀라게 하다
  If something astounds you, you are very surprised by it.

Build your Vocabulary

8. The Trunchbull

possess [pəzés] *v.* 소유하다, 가지고 있다
To have or own something, or to have a particular quality.

study [stʌ́di] *n.* 서재, (개인의) 연구실, 사무실; 공부, 연구; *v.* 배우다, 공부하다
A study is a room in a house which is used for reading, writing, and studying.

formidable [fɔ́:rmidəbəl] *a.* 무서운; 만만찮은, 얕잡을 수 없는; 굉장히 많은
Causing you to have fear or respect for something or someone because they are impressive, powerful or difficult.

sinewy [sínju:i] *a.* 힘줄의, 근골이 늠름한, 강건한; (문체가) 힘찬
Strong cord in the body connecting a muscle to a bone.

obstinate [obstinate] *a.* 완고한, 고집 센
Unreasonably determined, especially to act in a particular way and not to change at all, despite argument or persuasion.

arrogant [ǽrəgənt] *a.* 오만한, 건방진
Unpleasantly proud and behaving as if you are more important than, or know more than, other people.

odd [ɑd] *a.* 이상한, 기묘한
If you describe someone or something as odd, you think that they are strange or unusual.

smock [smɑk] *n.* (옷 위에 덧걸치는) 작업복, 덧입는 겉옷
A piece of clothing like a long shirt which is worn loosely over other clothing to protect it when working, or a piece of women's clothing that is similar to this.

pinch [pintʃ] *v.* (모자·구두 등이) 죄다, 꼭 끼다; 꼬집다; (문틈 등에) 끼다
To squeeze something, especially someone's skin, strongly between two hard things such as a finger and a thumb, usually causing pain.

thigh [θai] *n.* 넓적다리, 허벅다리
The part of a person's leg above the knee.

breech [bri:tʃ] *n.* 화포(火砲)의 꼬리 부분, 총개머리; 궁둥이

coarse [kɔ:rs] *a.* 조잡[악]한, 열등한; 거친, 올이 성긴; 야비한, 상스러운
Rough and not smooth or soft, or not in very small pieces.

Chapter 5-8

twill [twil] *n.* 능직(綾織), 능직물
A strong cotton cloth which has raised diagonal lines on the surface.

calf [kæf] *n.* 장딴지, 종아리
The thick curved part at the back of the human leg between the knee and the foot.

brogue [broug] *n.* 생가죽 신, 투박한 신, (구멍을 뚫어 장식한) 일상용화, 골프화
Brogues are thick leather shoes which have an elaborate pattern punched into the leather.

* **eccentric** [ikséntrik] *a.* (행동 따위가) 별난, 괴상한
Strange or unusual, sometimes in an amusing way.

bloodthirsty [blʌ́dθə̀ːrsti] *a.* 피에 굶주린; 살벌한, 잔인한
Wanting to kill or wound; enjoying seeing or hearing about killing and violence.

‡ **stag-hound** [stæg-haund] *n.* 스태그하운드(사슴 등을 사냥하던 큰 사냥개)

* **scowl** [skaul] *v.* 얼굴을 찌푸리다
To look at someone or something with a very annoyed expression.

c **fluster** [flʌ́stər] *v.* 당황하다, 혼란스럽게 하다
If you fluster someone, you make them upset and confused.

복습 **stinker** [stíŋkər] *n.* 불쾌한 놈, 골칫거리
Someone or something that is very unpleasant.

복습 **flick** [flik] *n.* (매·채찍 따위로) 찰싹[탁] 때리기; *v.* 찰싹[탁] 치다
To move or hit something with a short sudden movement.

spitball [spítbɔ̀ːl] *n.* (속어) 가벼운 비난; 종이를 씹어 뭉친 것
A piece of paper that has been chewed and then rolled into a ball to be thrown or shot at someone.

‡ **pillar** [pílər] *n.* 기둥, 대들보; 기둥 모양의 것
A strong column made of stone, metal or wood which supports part of a building.

J **brat** [bræt] *n.* (경멸적) 선머슴, 개구쟁이
A child, especially one who behaves badly.

c **wart** [wɔːrt] *n.* 사마귀
A small hard lump which grows on the skin, often on the face and hands.

Build your Vocabulary

- **darn** [dɑ:rn] ① *vt.* 감치다, 깁다, 꿰매다 ② (구어·완곡) damn
  Used instead of damn(=used to express anger or annoyance with someone or something) to express annoyance.

- **stink** [stíŋk] (stank(stunk)–stunk) *vi* 악취를 풍기다[풍기게 하다]; 평판이 나쁘다
  To smell very unpleasant.

- **sewer** ① [sú:ər] *n.* 하수구, 하수도 ② [souər] *n.* 바느질하는 사람, 재봉사
  A large pipe, usually underground, which is used for carrying waste water and human waste, such as urine and excrement.

  I'll be bound *idiom* (구어) 내가 장담한다, 틀림없다

- **squash** [skwɑʃ] *v.* 짓누르다, 으깨다
  To press something into a flatter shape, often breaking it.

  bluebottle [blú:bɑ̀tl] *n.* [곤충] 청파리

- **bang** [bæŋ] *v.* 탕 치다, 쾅 닫히다[닫다], 세게 치다
  To hit a part of the body accidentally against something.

  barmy [bá:rmi] *a.* 효모의, 발효 중의; (영·속어) 미친 사람 같은, 머리가 돈
  Behaving strangely, or very silly.

  bedbug [bédbʌ̀g] *n.* [곤충] 빈대
  A very small insect which lives mainly in beds and feeds by sucking people's blood.

- **resolutely** [rézəlù:tli] *a.* 굳게 결심한, 결연한, 굳은, 단호한
  Determined in character, action or ideas.

  browbeat [bráubì:t] *vt.* 위협하다, 을러대다, 호통치다; 위압하여 …하게 하다
  To try to force someone to do something by threatening them or using strong and unfair persuasion.

- **scorch** [skɔ:rtʃ] *v.* 태우다, 그슬리다
  To change colour with dry heat, or to burn slightly.

  knickers [níkərz] *n.* 여성용 내의
  A piece of women's underwear that covers the body from the waist to the tops of the legs.

  bullfrog [búlfrɑ̀g] *n.* [동물] 황소개구리
  A large North American frog that makes a loud, deep, rough noise.

* **snort** [snɔːrt] *v.* 콧김을 뿜다, 콧방귀 뀌다
To make an explosive sound by forcing air quickly up or down the nose.

piffle [pífəl] *n.* 바보 같은 짓, 쓸데없는 말(nonsense)
Nonsense.

twerp [twəːrp] *n.* (구어) 너절한 놈
A stupid person.

* **wretch** [retʃ] *n.* 가련한 사람; 철면피; 비열한 사람; (익살) (귀여운) 놈, 녀석
A person who experiences something unpleasant.

brigand [brígənd] *n.* 산적, 도적
An armed thief, especially one of a group living in the countryside and stealing from people travelling through the area.

* **viper** [váipər] *n.* 독사, 독사 같은 놈, 심지 나쁜 사람
A very unpleasant person whom you cannot trust.

* **birch** [bəːrtʃ] *n.* 자작나무로 만든 회초리
(the birch) The practice of hitting somebody with a bunch of birch sticks, as a punishment.

Crossword Puzzle

Use the clues and the words in the box to complete the crossword puzzle.

adore	precious	scorch	quiver	incapable coarse tip reluctantly
splendid	snort	fragile	crop	possess menace hunk purposely
devour	stink	formidable		

Chapter 5-8

Across

3 To love someone very much, especially in an admiring or respectful way, or to like something very much.
4 Excellent, or beautiful and impressive.
5 Unable to do something.
6 Intentionally.
8 To change colour with dry heat, or to burn slightly.
12 Rough and not smooth or soft, or not in very small pieces.
14 A plant such as a grain, fruit or vegetable grown in large amounts.
17 Not very willing to do something and therefore slow to do it.
19 Causing you to have fear or respect for something or someone because they are impressive, powerful or difficult.

Down

1 Easily damaged, broken or harmed.
2 Of great value because of being rare, expensive or important.
7 To make an explosive sound by forcing air quickly up or down the nose.
9 A large thick piece, especially of food.
10 To have or own something, or to have a particular quality.
11 Something or someone that is very annoying or troublesome.
13 To eat something eagerly and in large amounts so that nothing is left.
15 To shake slightly, often because of strong emotion.
16 To smell very unpleasant.
18 Move so that one side is higher than another side.

Comprehension Quiz

1. Parents normally think that their children _____.

A. are the best in the world

B. are nitwits

2. Why did Miss Honey want to visit the Wormwood's house at 9:00?

A. Because Matilda would be sleeping

B. Because the Wormwoods favorite TV show was on

C. Because it was not too late for a visit

D. Because she made an appointment

Chapter 9 **The Parents**

3. What did Mr. Wormwood think about her when he first saw Miss Honey?

A. She is a neighbor

B. She is Matilada's teacher

C. She is selling raffle tickets

D. She is the librarian

4. What did Mr. Wormwood say when he realized that Miss Honey was Matilda's teacher?

A. "If you can't talk sense then shut up."

B. "Oh my gawd!"

C. "You can't come in my house."

D. "Well, she's your responsibility from now on. You'll have to deal with her."

5. What does Mrs. Wormwood think of reading books? (two answers)

A. A girl doesn't get a man by being brainy

B. Looks are more important than books

C. I don't hold to book reading

D. You can't make a living sitting on your fanny reading books

Comprehension Quiz

1. What is not part of the Chokey?

A. Nails in the door

B. Glass on the walls

C. Ten inch square space to stand

D. Bright light shining in your eyes

2. What did Hortensia not do to Miss Trunchbull? (two answers)

A. She put Golden Syrup on the Trunchbull's seat

B. She put a frog in the water on the Trunchbull's desk

C. She put itching powder in the Trunchbull's underwear

D. She put a stink bomb in the Trunchbull's office

3. What happened to Julius Rottwinkle?

A. Miss Trunchbull forced him to eat all of the chocolate cake

B. Miss Trunchbull ordered him go and stand in the corner on one leg with his face to the wall

C. Miss Trunchbull threw him out of the window

D. Miss Trunchbull slapped him on the cheek

4. What is the Trunchbull's favorite sport?

A. Football

B. Wrestling

C. Hammer throw

D. Sumo

Chapter 10 **Throwing the Hammer**

5. Why did the Trunchbull throw Amanda over the fence?

A. Because Amanda was wearing pig tails

B. Because she talked back

C. Because the Trunchbull wanted some exercise

D. Because Amanda was in the wrong school

Comprehension Quiz

1. How can Miss Trunchbull get away with her outrageous behavior? (two answers)
A. The parents are afraid to object because the Trunchbull is too scary
B. The parents don't care as long as the children go to school
C. The parents don't know what is happening in the school
D. The parents would never believe the crazy stories that the children would tell

2. What did Bruce Bogtrotter steal?
A. The Trunchbull's candies
B. A piece of chocolate cake
C. The cook's tea tray
D. A puzzle

3. What does the cook look like?
A. Short, thin, old, and frail
B. Like all of her body juices had been dried out in an oven
C. Looked as though her mouth was full of lemon juice
D. Looked like she had not showered this century

4. How big is the cake that the cook brings out?
(A)_____

Chapter 11 **Bruce Bogtrotter and the Cake**

5. Put the events in order. (-   -   -   )

A. Bruce finished the cake and grinned

B. The Trunchbull screamed and marched away

C. The Trunchbull broke the china platter on Bruce's head

D. All of the students cheered

Comprehension Quiz

1. What must the children not do when the Trunchbull comes to class?
A. Wash their faces and hands
B. Sing a song
C. Stand up when you answer a question
D. Learn your spelling words and two times tables

2. Why did Lavender want to be a hero?
A. Because of the stories she heard from Miss Honey
B. Because she likes heroes
C. Because she wants to fight the Trunchbull
D. Because of a story she heard from Hortensia and Matilda

3. What was Lavender's job?
A. To make a cookies for the Trunchbull
B. To clean the classroom
C. To place a jug of water and glass on the table for the Headmistress
D. To introduce her class to the Headmistress

4. What is her plan?
(A)_____

Chapter 12 **Lavender**

Build your Vocabulary

9. The Parents

seek [si:k] (sought-sought) *v.* 찾다, 추구하다, 얻으려 하다
To try to find or get something, especially something which is not a physical object.

stuck-up [stʌkʌ̀p] *a.* (구어) 거드름부리는, 점잔빼는, 거만한
If you say that someone is stuck-up, you mean that are very proud and unfriendly because they think they are very important.

reassemble [rì:əsémbəl] *v.* 다시 모으다[모이다]; 새로 짜 맞추다
If a group of people reassembles or if you reassemble them, they gather together again in a group.

presume [prizú:m] *vt.* 추정하다, 상상하다, 생각하다
To believe something to be true because it is very likely, although you are not certain.

nigh [nai] *a., ad., prep.* [고어·시어·방언] =NEAR
Near; almost, nearly.

offspring [ɔ́(:)fspriŋ] *n.* (pl.) 자식, 자녀들; 자손, 후예
A person's children.

nitwit [nitwit] *n.* 바보, 멍청이
A foolish or stupid person.

precisely [prisáisli] *ad.* 정밀하게, 정확히, 정확하게
Exactly.

cosy [kóuzi] (=cozy) *a.* (방 등이) (따뜻하여) 기분 좋은, 편안한; 아늑한
Comfortable and pleasant, especially because small and warm.

nook [nuk] *n.* (방 따위의) 구석, 모퉁이, 쑥 들어간 곳, 외진 곳, 피난처, 숨는 곳
A small space which is hidden or partly sheltered.

nosey cook 'cosy nook'과 운을 맞춘 것으로, 번역서에는 'cosy nook-nosey cook'을 '아담한 오두막-암담한 부뚜막'으로 번역하고 있다.

ratty [rǽti] *a.* 쥐 같은, 쥐 특유의; (영·속어) 성마른, 성을 잘 내는
Easily annoyed; irritable.

moustache [mʌ́stæʃ] (=mustache) *n.* (미) 코밑수염, 동물의 수염
Hair which a man grows above his upper lip.

Chapter 9-12

raffle [rǽfəl] *n.* 복권 판매
An activity in which people buy numbered tickets, some of which are later chosen to win prizes, which is arranged in order to make money for a good social purpose.

butt in *idiom* (구어) …에 참견하다, 주제넘게 나서다
If you say that someone is butting in, you are criticizing the fact that they are joining in a conversation or activity without being asked to.

startle [stá:rtl] *v.* 깜짝 놀라다
If something startles you, it surprises and frightens you slightly.

darn [dɑ:rn] ① *v.* 감치다, 깁다, 꿰매다 ② (구어·완곡) damn
Used instead of damn(=used to express anger or annoyance with someone or something) to express annoyance.

frail [freil] *a.* 약한, 부서지기 쉬운, 무른
Weak or unhealthy, or easily damaged, broken or harmed.

resolutely [rézəlù:tli] *a.* 굳게 결심한, 결연한, 굳은, 단호한
Determined in character, action or ideas.

porch [pɔ:rtʃ] *n.* 현관, 포치, 차대는 곳, 입구
A covered structure in front of the entrance to a building.

briskly [brískli] *ad.* 활발히, 팔팔하게, 세차게, 상쾌히, 기분 좋게
Quick, energetic and active.

rapturous [rǽptʃərəs] *a.* 기뻐 날뛰는, 미칠 듯이 기뻐하는, 열광적인
(**rapturously** *ad.* 기뻐서, 열광적으로)
A rapturous feeling or reaction is one of extreme happiness or enthusiasm.

juggle [dʒʌ́gəl] *v.* 요술을 부리다; 저글(공 세 개를 공중에서 돌리는 묘기)을 하다
To throw a set of three or more objects such as balls into the air and catch and throw them again quickly, one at a time.

daft [dæft] *a.* (영·구어) 어리석은; 미친, 발광하는
Silly or stupid.

fanny [fǽni] (미·속어) 엉덩이
Someone's fanny is their bottom.

intrigue [intrí:g] *vt.* …의 호기심을 돋우다; *vi.* 음모를 꾸미다; *n.* 음모
If something intrigues you, it interests you and you want to know more about it.

Build your Vocabulary

plump [plʌmp] *a.* 부푼, 풍만한, 살이 찐
Having a pleasantly soft rounded body or shape.

smug [smʌg] *a.* 잘난 체하는, 거만한 (smugly *ad.* 잘난 체하며)
Too pleased or satisfied about something you have achieved or something you know.

suet [súːət] *n.* 소[양] 기름
A type of hard fat used in cooking which is taken from around the kidneys of such animals as sheep and cows.

nasty [nǽsti] *a.* 더러운, 불쾌한, 몹시 싫은; 심술궂은, 험악한
Bad or very unpleasant.

simper [símpər] *v.* 억지웃음을 웃다, 선웃음 치다
To smile in a foolish or silly way.

sloppy [slápi] *a.* 질퍽한, 물이 많이 괸; (구어) 너절한
(sloppiness *n.* 물기가 많음; 맛 없음)
Containing too much liquid.

bosomy [búzəmi] *a.* 도도록이 솟아 오른; (여자가) 가슴이 풍만한
Describes a woman with large breasts.

craggy [krǽgi] *a.* 바위가 많은, 울퉁불퉁하고 험한
Describe a man's face that is quite roughly formed and has loose skin but is also attractive.

delinquent [dilíkwənt] *n.* 태만한 사람, 범법자, 비행 소년
A person, usually young, who behaves in a way that is illegal or unacceptable to most people.

flesh [fleʃ] *n.* 살, 육체
The soft part of the body of a person or animal which is between the skin and the bones, or the soft inner part of a fruit or vegetable.

sue [suː] *v.* 고소하다, 소송을 제기하다
To take legal action against a person or organization, especially by making a legal claim for money because of some harm that they have caused you.

despise [dispáiz] *vt.* 경멸하다, 멸시하다
To feel a strong dislike for someone or something because you think they are bad or worthless.

10. Throwing the Hammer

gormless [gɔ́ːrmlis] *a.* (영·속어) 얼뜬, 아둔한
Stupid and slow to understand.

wrap up *phrasal v.* (물건을) 싸다; (참뜻을) …에 숨기고 표현하다
To cover or enclose something in paper, cloth or other material.

overmuch [óuvərmʌ́tʃ] *a.* 과다한, 과분한; *ad.* 과도하게
Too much or very much.

nymph [nimf] *n.* [그리스·로마신화] 님프 (자연물에 깃든 소녀 모습의 정령)
A goddess or spirit in the form of a young woman, living in a tree, river, mountain, etc.

fringe [frindʒ] *n.* (숄·테이블 가장자리의) 술, 술 장식; 가장자리, 부차적인 것
The outer or less important part of an area, group or activity.

gutsy [gʌ́tsi] *a.* (구어) 기운찬, 용감한; (록 음악 따위) 강한 감동을 주는
With sudden, strong winds.

rugged [rʌ́gid] *a.* 울퉁불퉁한; 바위투성이의; (얼굴이) 주름진, 못생긴
Strong and simple; not delicate.

scum [skʌm] *n.* (액체 표면에) 떠 있는 찌끼, 거품; 인간쓰레기, 더러운 놈
A very bad or immoral person or group of people.

crisp [krisp] *n.* (pl.) (영) 얇게 썬 감자 프라이, 포테이토 칩; 아삭아삭한; 또렷한
A thin round slice of potato that is fried until hard then dried and eaten cold.

confront [kənfrʌ́nt] *vt.* 직면하다, 마주 대하다; 대조하다
To face, meet or deal with a difficult situation or person.

loathe [louð] *vt.* 몹시 싫어하다, 진저리를 내다; 지겨워하다
To be unwilling to do something.

grub [grʌb] *n.* 굼벵이, 구더기, 유충
An insect in the stage when it has just come out of its egg.

hatch [hætʃ] *vt.* (알을) 까다, 부화시키다
To (cause an egg to) break in order to allow a young animal to come out.

crumb [krʌm] *n.* 작은 조각, 빵 부스러기, 빵가루
A very small piece of bread, cake or biscuit.

Build your Vocabulary

titchy *a.* (영) 체구가 작은
Extremely small.

regale [rigéil] *v.* 기쁘게 해주다, 만족케 하다; 융숭하게 대접하다, 향응하다
To entertain someone with stories, jokes, etc.

★ **mistrust** [mistrʌ́st] *vt.* 신용하지 않다, 의심하다
To have doubts about the honesty or abilities of someone.

J ★ **squat** [skwɔt] *a.* 웅크린, 쭈그린; 땅딸막한; *vi.* 웅크리다, 쭈그리다
To sit on your heels with your knees bent up close to your body.

wobble [wábəl] *v.* 흔들리다, 동요하다, 떨리다
To shake or move from side to side in a way that shows a lack of balance.

‡ **tin** [tin] *n.* 주석, 양철 깡통[냄비]
A metal container in which food and drink is sold.

J **squelch** [skweltʃ] *v.* 짓누르다, 찌그러뜨리다; 철벅철벅 소리나게 하다
To make a sucking sound like the one produced when you are walking on soft wet ground.

★ **hippopotamus** [hìpəpátəməs] *n.* [동물] 하마
A very large animal with short legs and thick, dark grey skin which lives near water in Africa.

★ **amiably** [éimiəbli] *ad.* 상냥하게, 친절하게, 온화하게
Describes a person or their behaviour that is pleasant and friendly.

복 **breech** [bri:tʃ] *n.* 화포(火砲)의 꼬리 부분, 총개머리; 궁둥이

‡ **clasp** [klæsp] *v.* 고정시키다, 죄다; 꼭 쥐다, 악수하다; *n.* 걸쇠, 버클; 악수, 포옹
To hold someone or something firmly in your hands or arms.

muck [mʌk] *n.* 쓰레기, 오물, 더러운 것; 거름, 퇴비
Dirt or animal excrement.

C 복 **squirt** [skwə:rt] *n.* (구어) 건방진 벼락부자[젊은이]; 꼬마; *v.* 분출시키다, 뿜다
A young or small person whom you consider to be unimportant and who has behaved rudely towards you.

C ★ **sneak** [sni:k] *v.* 몰래[살금살금] 움직이다
If you sneak somewhere, you go there very quietly on foot, trying to avoid being seen.

Chapter 9-12

- **gulp** [gʌlp] *v.* 꿀꺽꿀꺽 마시다, 쭉 삼켜버리다
  To eat or drink food or liquid quickly by swallowing it in large amounts, or to make a swallowing movement because of fear, surprise or excitement.

- **babble** [bǽbəl] *v.* 실없이 지껄이다, 불명료한 소리를 내다
  To talk or say something in a quick, confused, excited way.

- **bog** [bɑg] *n.* 습지, 수렁; *v.* 수렁에 빠뜨리다[빠지다]
  Soft, wet earth, or an area of this.

- **knickers** [níkərz] *n.* 여성용 내의
  A piece of women's underwear that covers the body from the waist to the tops of the legs.

- **spellbound** [spélbàund] *a.* 마법에 걸린, 넋을 잃은
  Extremely interested in something.

- **itching** [itʃiŋ] *n.* 가려움; 하고 싶어 못 견딤; *a.* 가려운; …하고 싶어 못 견디는
  To have or cause an uncomfortable feeling on the skin which makes you want to rub it with your nails.

- **welt** [welt] *n.* 채찍 자국, (매질 등으로) 부푼 자리; (속어) 심한 구타
  A raised, red area of skin caused by being hit or by cuts healing.

- **cram** [kræm] *v.* 억지로 채워 넣다, 밀어 넣다
  To force a lot of things into a small space, or to do many things in a short period of time.

- **wasp** [wɑsp] *n.* 장수말벌; 성질 잘 내는 사람
  A black and yellow flying insect which can sting you.

- **leap** [li:p] (leapt-leapt) *v.* 껑충 뛰다, 뛰어넘다; *n.* 뜀, 도약, 비약, 급변
  To make a large jump or sudden movement, usually from one place to another.

- **enthrall** [enθrɔ́:l] *v.* 매혹하다, 마음을 빼앗다, 사로잡다, 노예(상태)로 하다
  To keep someone completely interested.

- **skulduggery** [skʌldʌ́gəri] *n.* (구어·우스개) 야바위, 속임수, 음모, 부정
  Secret and dishonest behaviour.

- **limb** [lim] *n.* 팔다리, 날개; 큰 가지; 돌출부
  An arm or leg of a person or animal, or a large branch of a tree.

Build your Vocabulary

- **pursuit** [pərsúːt] *n.* 추적, 추격, 추구
  The act of chasing or pursuing.

- **blemish** [blémiʃ] *n.* 흠, 오점, 결점
  A fault in a person's character.

- **culprit** [kʌ́lprit] *n.* 죄인, 범죄자
  Someone who has done something wrong.

- **torture** [tɔ́ːrtʃər] *n.* 고문, 고뇌; *vt.* 고문하다, 고통을 주다
  The act of causing great physical or mental pain in order to persuade someone to do something or to give information, or as an act of cruelty to a person or animal.

- **overawe** [òuvərɔ́ː] *vt.* 위압하다; 겁을 주어 …하게 하다
  To cause someone to feel a mixture of extreme respect and fear.

- **casualty** [kǽʒuəlti] *n.* 사고, 재난, 상해; 사상자, 희생자, 부상자
  A person injured or killed in a serious accident or war.

- **crusader** [kruːséidər] *n.* 십자군 전사, 개혁 운동가
  A person who takes part in a crusade.

- **gallant** [ɡǽlənt] *a.* 씩씩한, 용감한; *n.* 씩씩한 사람, 멋쟁이; *v.* 친절히 하다
  Showing no fear of dangerous or difficult things.

- **foul** [faul] *a.* 더러운, 불결한, 냄새 나는; 비열한, 음험한, 못된
  Extremely unpleasant.

- **serpent** [sə́ːrpənt] *n.* 뱀 (특히 크고 독 있는 종류); 뱀 같은 사람
  A snake.

- **scripture** [skríptʃər] *n.* 성서, 경전; 성서의 한 절, 성구
  The holy writings of a religion.

- **ruddy** [rʌ́di] *a.* 붉은, 불그스름한; (영·속어) 싫은, 괘씸한
  Used to avoid saying bloody to express anger or annoyance.

- **whisk** [hwisk] *v.* (먼지 등을) 털다, 털어내다; 휙 움직이다
  To take something or someone somewhere else suddenly and quickly.

- **menace** [ménəs] *n.* (구어) 골칫거리, 말썽꾸러기; 협박, 공갈
  Something or someone that is very annoying or troublesome.

Chapter 9-12

formidable [fɔ́ːrmidəbəl] *a.* 무서운; 만만찮은, 얕잡을 수 없는; 굉장히 많은
Causing you to have fear or respect for something or someone because they are impressive, powerful or difficult.

breech [briːtʃ] *n.* 화포(火砲)의 꼬리 부분, 총개머리; 궁둥이

plait [pleit] *vt.* 닿다, 엮다, 접다, …에 주름잡다
If you plait three or more lengths of hair, rope, or other material together, you twist them over and under each other to make one thick length.

filthy [fílθi] *a.* 불결한, 더러운
Extremely or unpleasantly dirty.

pigtail [pígtèil] *n.* 땋아 늘인 머리 (돼지 꼬리와 비슷한 모양에서 유래)
A length of hair which is tied at the back of the head or at each side of the head, sometimes in a plait.

dustbin [dʌ́stbìn] *n.* (영) 쓰레기통
A large container for rubbish from a house or other building, usually made of strong plastic or metal and kept outside.

paralyse [pǽrəlàiz] *vt.* 마비시키다; 무력[무능]하게 만들다; 쓸모없게 만들다
To cause a person, animal or part of the body to lose the ability to move or feel.

stutter [stʌ́tər] *v.* 말을 더듬다, 더듬거리며 말하다
To speak or say something, especially the first part of a word, with difficulty, for example pausing before it or repeating it several times.

twit [twit] *n.* 바보
A stupid person.

bellow [bélou] *vi.* 큰 소리로 울다; 고함지르다
To shout in a loud voice, or (of a cow or large animal) to make a loud, deep sound.

blancmange [bləmάːndʒ] *n.* 블라망주(우유로 만든 디저트의 일종)
A cold sweet food made from milk, sugar and corn flour.

toot [tuːt] *n.* (나팔·피리 등을) 불기, 부는 소리; 경적; *v.* 나팔·피리 등을 불다; 경적을 울리다
A short high sound made by a car horn or a whistle.

lunge [lʌndʒ] *vi.* 찌르다, 돌진하다, 치다
To move forward suddenly and with force.

Build your Vocabulary

scream blue murder *idiom* (구어) 비명 지르다, 큰일났다고 소리 지르다

★ **pivot** [pívət] *v.* (…을 추축으로) 회전하다, 선회하다
To turn or balance on a central point.

★ **blur** [blə:r] *n.* 더러움, 얼룩; 결점, 오점, 오명; 흐림, 불선명
Something that you cannot see clearly.

복습 **grunt** [grʌnt] *v.* (돼지가) 꿀꿀거리다, 툴툴거리다
To make a short low sound instead of speaking, usually because of anger or pain.

mesmerize [mésməràiz] *vt.* (꼼짝 못할 정도로) 놀라게 하다; 최면술을 걸다
To have someone's attention completely so that they cannot think of anything else.

※ **descend** [disénd] *v.* 내려가다, 내리다
To go or come down.

parabola [pəræbələ] *n.* [수학] 포물선; 파라볼라
A type of curve such as that made by an object that is thrown up in the air and falls to the ground in a different place.

※ **daze** [deiz] *v.* 멍하게[아찔하게] 하다; 현혹시키다, 눈부시게 하다; *n.* 멍한 상태
Very confused and unable to think clearly because you are shocked or have hit your head.

★ **totter** [tátər] *vi.* 비틀거리다, 기우뚱거리다
To walk in a shaky way that looks as if you are about to fall.

11. Bruce Bogtrotter and the Cake

★ **stink** [stíŋk] (stank(stunk)-stunk) *vi.* 악취를 풍기다[풍기게 하다]; 평판이 나쁘다
To smell very unpleasant.

★ **halves** [hævz] *n.* half의 복수
Either of the two equal or nearly equal parts that together make up a whole.

★ **outrageous** [autréidʒəs] *a.* 난폭한, 잔인무도한
Shocking and morally unacceptable.

★ **hog** [hɔ:g] *n.* (미) (식용) 돼지; (구어) 돼지 같은 놈, 욕심꾸러기
Someone who takes much more than a fair share of something, especially by eating too much.

Chapter 9-12

upturned [ʌptə́:rnd] *a.* (시선 등이) 치뜬; 끝이 위로 향한; 뒤집힌; 파헤쳐진
Pointing or looking up, or having the part which is usually at the bottom turned to be at the top.

waddle [wάdl] *vi.* 뒤뚱거리며 걷다, 어기적어기적 걷다
To walk with short steps, swinging the body from one side to the other.

briskly [brískli] *ad.* 활발히, 팔팔하게, 세차게, 상쾌히, 기분 좋게
Quick, energetic and active.

wary [wέəri] *a.* 경계하는, 주의 깊은, 신중한
Not completely trusting or certain about something or someone.

shuffle [ʃʌ́fl] *v.* (발을) 질질 끌다; 이리저리 움직이다
To move or drag (one's feet) with short quick sliding steps.

plump [plʌmp] *a.* 부푼, 풍만한, 살이 찐
Having a pleasantly soft rounded body or shape.

flabby [flǽbi] *a.* (몸에 살이 쪄서) 흐늘흐늘 하는, 축 늘어진
Soft and fat, weak.

clot [klɑt] *n.* (엉긴) 덩어리, 떼; *v.* 덩어리지다, 응고하다
An almost solid lump.

rapier [réipiər] *n.* 가볍고 가느다란 칼의 일종 (찌르기를 주로 한 결투용)
A sword with a long thin blade.

carbuncle [kά:rbʌŋkəl] *n.* [의학] 등창, 여드름, 뾰루지; [광물] 홍옥(紅玉)
A large painful swelling under the skin.

pustule [pʌ́stʃu:l] *n.* [의학] 고름 물집; [동·식물] 작은 융기
A small raised area on the skin which contains pus.

denizen [dénəzən] *n.* 주민, 거주자
An animal, plant or person that lives in or is often in a particular place.

genuinely [dʒinjuinəli] *ad.* 진정으로, 성실하게; 순수하게
If people or emotions are genuine, they are honest and sincere.

crook [kruk] *n.* 갈고리; (구어) 사기꾼, 도둑; *v.* 구부리다; 훔치다
If you crook your arm or finger, you bend it.

Build your Vocabulary

C ★ **pirate** [páiərət] *n.* 해적, 해적선, 약탈자; *v.* 약탈하다
A person who sails in a ship and attacks other ships in order to steal from them.

복습 **brigand** [brígənd] *n.* 산적, 도적
An armed thief, especially one of a group living in the countryside and stealing from people travelling through the area.

rustler [rʌ́slər] *n.* (미·구어) 소도둑; 살랑살랑 소리를 내는 것, 활동가
A person who steals farm animals.

gumboil [gʌ́mbɔ̀il] *n.* 잇몸 궤양

★ **plead** [pli:d] *v.* 변호하다, 변론하다; 탄원하다, 간청하다
To make an urgent, emotional statement or request for something.

suppurate [sʌ́pjərèit] *vi.* 곪다, 화농(化膿)하다
To form or give out a thick yellow liquid because of infection.

복습 **serpent** [sə́:rpənt] *n.* 뱀 (특히 크고 독 있는 종류); 뱀 같은 사람
A snake.

복습 **filth** [filθ] *n.* 오물, 불결한 물건, 쓰레기, 더러움
Thick, unpleasant dirt.

★ **robber** [rábər] *n.* 강도, 도둑
Someone who steals.

★ **bandit** [bǽndit] *n.* 산적, 노상강도, 도둑; 악당, 무법자
An armed thief, especially one belonging to a group that attack people travelling through the countryside.

J **fleck** [flek] *n.* 반점, 얼룩, 주근깨
A small mark or spot.

CJ ★ **froth** [frɔ:θ] *n.* 거품 *v.* 거품을 일으키다
To have or produce a lot of small bubbles which often rise to the surface.

CJ ★ **mumble** [mʌ́mbəl] *v.* 중얼거리다, 웅얼거리다; 우물우물 씹다; *n.* 중얼거림
To speak unclearly and quietly so that the words are difficult to understand.

★ **inhabit** [inhǽbit] *vt.* …에 살다, …에 거주하다
To live in a place.

Chapter 9-12

CJ ★ **shrivel** [ʃríːvəl] *v.* 주름(살)지다[지게 하다], 줄어들다
To become dry, smaller and covered with lines as if by crushing or folding, or to make something do this.

‡ **forbid** [fərbíd] (forbade-forbidden) *vt.* 금하다, 허락하지 않다
To refuse to allow something, especially officially, or to prevent a particular plan of action by making it impossible.

CJ ★ **smack** [smæk] *vt.* 찰싹 치다; *n.* 찰싹 하는 소리
To hit something hard against something else so that it makes a short loud noise.

J ‡ **thigh** [θai] *n.* 넓적다리
The part of a person's leg above the knee.

C ‡ **stagger** [stǽgər] *v.* 비틀거리다[게 하다]; 흔들리다[게 하다]
To walk or move with a lack of balance as if you are going to fall.

bemuse [bimjúːz] *vt.* 멍하게 하다, 곤혹케 하다, 생각에 잠기게 하다
If something bemuses you, it puzzles or confuses you.

bootlace [búːtlèis] *n.* (영) 구두끈
A long thin cord or strip of leather used to fasten boots.

implacable [implǽkəbəl] *a.* (적·증오심 등이) 달래기 어려운; 준엄한
Describes (someone who has) strong opinions or feelings which are impossible to change.

J ★ **crafty** [krǽfti] *a.* 교활한, 간악한, 교묘한, 능란한
If you describe someone as crafty, you mean that they achieve what they want in a clever way, especially by indirect or dishonest methods.

★ **tense** [tens] *a.* 팽팽한, 긴장한, 긴박한; *v.* 팽팽하게 하다, 긴장시키다[하다]
Nervous and anxious and unable to relax.

arsenic [άːrsénik] *n.* 비소 (비금속 원소로 독성을 가지고 있음); *a.* 비소의
A very poisonous element, often used to kill rats and able to kill people.

gingerly [dʒíndʒərli] *ad.* 지극히 조심스럽게, 주의 깊게
In a way that is careful or cautious.

CJ ‡ **peculiar** [pikjúːljər] *a.* 기묘한, 이상한; 특이한, 눈에 띄는
Unusual and strange, sometimes in an unpleasant way.

Build your Vocabulary

- **belch** [beltʃ] *v.* 분출하다, 내뿜다; 트림을 하다; *n.* 트림 (소리); 폭발(음)
  To allow air from the stomach to come out noisily through the mouth.

- **giggle** [gígəl] *v.* 킥킥 웃다
  To laugh repeatedly in a quiet but uncontrolled and childish way.

- **flag** [flæg] ① *n.* 기, 깃발 ② *v.* (활력·활동·흥미 등이) 떨어지다; 시들해지다
  To become tired or less interested.

- **subtle** [sʌ́tl] *a.* 미묘한, 포착하기 힘든, 희미한
  Not loud, bright, noticeable or obvious in any way.

- **impend** [impénd] *vi.* (위험·사건 따위가) 절박하다, 바야흐로 일어나려 하다
  Describes an event, usually something unpleasant or unwanted, that is going to happen soon.

- **disaster** [dizǽstər] *n.* 재해, 참사
  A very bad accident such as an earthquake or a plane crash.

- **gill** [gil] *n.* (보통 pl.) 아가미; (구어·익살) 턱과 귀밑의 군살
  The organ through which fish and other water creatures breathe.

- **surrender** [səréndər] *v.* 항복하다, 내어주다, 넘겨주다; *n.* 항복, 굴복
  To stop fighting and admit defeat.

- **mercy** [mə́ːrsi] *n.* 자비, 연민
  Kindness and forgiveness shown towards someone whom you have authority over.

- **jolly** [dʒáli] *a.* 명랑한, 즐거운, 유쾌한; *ad.* (영·구어) 대단히, 몹시
  very.

- **wheel** [hwiːl] *v.* 방향을 바꾸다, 선회하다; (수레바퀴 달린 것을) 움직이다, 밀다
  If you wheel an object that has wheels somewhere, you push it along.

- **intently** [inténtli] *ad.* 골똘하게, 여념 없이, 오로지
  Giving all your attention to something.

- **dogged** [dɔ́(ː)gid] *a.* 완강한, 끈질긴, 집요한
  Very determined to do something, even if it is very difficult.

- **perseverance** [pə̀ːrsivíːrəns] *n.* 인내(력), 참을성
  Continued effort and determination.

Chapter 9-12

- **grub** [grʌb] *n.* 굼벵이, 구더기, 유충
  An insect in the stage when it has just come out of its egg.

- **replete** [riplí:t] *a.* 가득 찬, 충만한, 충분한; 포만한, 포식한
  Full, especially with food.

- **comatose** [kóumətòus] *a.* [의학] 혼수성의, 혼수상태의
  Extremely tired and lacking in energy; sleeping deeply.

- **bead** [bi:d] *n.* 구슬, 유리알, (이슬·땀 따위의) 방울; *v.* 구슬로 장식하다
  A small coloured often round piece of plastic, wood, glass, etc. with a hole through it. It is usually put on a string with a lot of others to make jewellery.

- **lunge** [lʌndʒ] *vi.* 찌르다, 돌진하다, 치다
  To move forward suddenly and with force.

- **sackful** [sǽkfùl] *n.* 부대 가득한 분량, 한 부대, 한 섬, 다량
  The amount contained in a sack.

- **Go to blazes!** *idiom* 빌어먹을, 뒈져라
  Used to tell someone to go away.

12. Lavender

- **chirrup** [tʃírəp] *v.* 지저귀다
  To make a short high sound or sounds.

- **swot** [swɑt] *v.* 맹렬히 공부하다, 들이 파다
  To study very hard, especially in order to prepare for an exam.

- **scheme** [ski:m] *n.* 계획, 기획, 설계
  An officially organized plan or system.

- **heroic** [hiróuik] *a.* 영웅[용사]의; 용맹스러운, 씩씩한
  Very brave or great.

- **deed** [di:d] *n.* 행위, 실행, 사실
  An intentional act, especially a very bad or very good one.

- **swear** [swɛər] (swore–sworn) *v.* 맹세하다; …에게 욕을 하다; …라고 단언하다
  To state or promise that you are telling the truth or that you will do something or behave in a particular way.

Build your Vocabulary

come up with *idiom* …에 따라잡다; …에 복수하다; (구어) 제안하다, 고안하다
To reach the usual or necessary standard.

mull [mʌl] *n.* 실수, 실패, 혼란; *v.* 엉망으로 만들다, 실패하다
To think carefully about something for a long time.

germ [dʒəːrm] *n.* 세균, 병원균
A very small organism that causes disease.

admittedly [ædmítədli] *ad.* 일반적으로; 틀림없이, 확실히
Used when you are agreeing that something is true, especially unwillingly.

formidable [fɔ́ːrmidəbəl] *a.* 무서운; 만만찮은, 얕잡을 수 없는; 굉장히 많은
Causing you to have fear or respect for something or someone because they are impressive, powerful or difficult.

foe [fou] *n.* 적, 원수
An enemy.

secrecy [síːkrəsi] *n.* 비밀; 비밀 엄수
A piece of information that is only known by one person or a few people and should not be told to others.

exploit [éksplɔit] *vt.* 개척[개발]하다; (부당하게) 이용하다; (노동력을) 착취하다
To use someone or something unfairly for your own advantage.

newt [njuːt] *n.* [동물] 영원(도롱뇽과의 총칭); (미·속어) 바보, 멍청이
A small animal which has a long thin body and tail and short legs, and lives both on land and in water.

murky [mə́ːrki] *a.* 어두운, (안개·연기가) 자욱한
Dark and difficult to see through.

amphibian [æmfíbiən] *n.* 양서 동물
An animal, such as a frog, which lives both on land and in water but must lay its eggs in water.

whopper [hwápər] *n.* (구어) 때리는 사람; 엄청난 것; 새빨간 거짓말, 허풍
Something that is surprising because it is so much bigger than the usual size.

wriggle [rígəl] *v.* 꿈틀거리다, 몸부림치다; *n.* 몸부림침, 꿈틀거림
To twist your body, or move part of your body, with small, quick movements.

Chapter 9-12

squirm [skwə:rm] *v.i.* (벌레처럼) 꿈틀거리다, 움직거리다, 꿈틀거리며 나아가다
To move from side to side in an awkward way because of nervousness, embarrassment or pain.

★ **quicksilver** [kwíksìlvər] *n.* 수은; 쾌활한[변덕스러운] 성질, 변덕스러운 사람
Quicksilver movements or changes are very fast and unpredictable.

★ **satchel** [sǽtʃəl] *n.* 작은 가방, 학생 가방
A rectangular leather bag with a long strap, used especially in the past by children for carrying books to school.

C **tingle** [tíŋgəl] *v.* 따끔따끔 아프다, 얼얼하게 하다; 설레다[게 하다], 울렁거리다
To have a feeling as if a lot of sharp points are being put quickly and lightly into your body.

C 복습 **culprit** [kʌ́lprit] *n.* 죄인, 범죄자
Someone who has done something wrong.

plop [plɑp] *n.* 풍덩, 쿵, 퐁당 (소리); 풍덩 (떨어짐)
A soft sound like that of something solid dropping lightly into a liquid.

Crossword Puzzle

Use the clues and the words in the box to complete the crossword puzzle.

froth	murky	mumble	lunge	stutter	totter	stagger	startle
belch	subtle	exploit	culprit	peculiar	swear	tense	crafty
presume	blur	gallant	surrender				

Across

3 To speak unclearly and quietly so that the words are difficult to understand.
5 Unusual and strange, sometimes in an unpleasant way.
6 Something that you cannot see clearly.
8 Showing no fear of dangerous or difficult things.
12 To stop fighting and admit defeat.
13 To walk in a shaky way that looks as if you are about to fall.
17 To speak or say something, especially the first part of a word, with difficulty, for example pausing before it or repeating it several times.
18 To believe something to be true because it is very likely, although you are not certain.
19 Not loud, bright, noticeable or obvious in any way.

Down

1 To state or promise that you are telling the truth or that you will do something or behave in a particular way.
2 To allow air from the stomach to come out noisily through the mouth.
3 Dark and difficult to see through.
4 To use someone or something unfairly for your own advantage.
7 Someone who has done something wrong.
9 To move forward suddenly and with force.
10 If you describe someone as crafty, you mean that they achieve what they want in a clever way, especially by indirect or dishonest methods.
11 To walk or move with a lack of balance as if you are going to fall.
14 Nervous and anxious and unable to relax.
15 If something _____s you, it surprises and frightens you slightly.
16 To have or produce a lot of small bubbles which often rise to the surface.

Comprehension Quiz

1. Why is Miss Trunchbull angry at Nigel Hicks? (two answers)

A. His hands are dirty

B. His father is a doctor

C. He has lunch on his shirt

D. He makes noise

2. How do the children learn to spell?

(A)_____

3. What does Miss Trunchbull do to Rupert?

A. She kicks his chair

B. She said good things about him

C. She makes him sing a song

D. She picks him up by his hair

4. What does Miss Trunchbull do to Eric Ink?

A. She picks him up by his eyebrows

B. She picks him up by his fingers

C. She picks him up by his nose

D. She picks him up by his ears

Chapter 13 **The Weekly Test**

5. What does Miss Trunchbull think is the best way to teach?

A. Explain ideas to the students

B. Teach spelling with poetry

C. Hammer the ideas into the children

D. Stretch out their ears

6. What does Miss Trunchbull think of clever people?

(A)_____

Comprehension Quiz

1. How does the Trunchbull want to get rid of all of the students? (two answers)

A. Sticky paper to collect all of the students

B. Open a school with no student

C. Spray to kill all of the students

D. Make take tests until they die

2. What do students not think is in the glass?

A. A crocodile

B. A frog

C. A snake

D. An alligator

3. What does the Trunchbull not threaten to do to Matilda?

A. Put her in a reform school for forty years

B. Drum her out of the school

C. Have prefects chase her out with hockey sticks

D. Throw her over the fence by her pigtails

4. What emotion helped Matilda find her power?

A. Sadness

B. Calm

C. Anger

D. Desperation

Chapter 14 **The First Miracle**

5. Where was Matilda's power located?

A. In her head

B. In her hands

C. In her heart

D. In her eyes

Comprehension Quiz

1. What does Matilda tell Miss Honey?

A. I broke the glass with my eyes

B. I bent the spoon with my fingers

C. I knocked over the glass with my eyes

D. I sliced an apple into two with my hands

2. What does Miss Honey say when the glass topples over a second time? (two answers)

A. That is amazing

B. I don't believe it

C. How did you do that?

D. It is not possible

3. What did Matilda notice about the second time?

A. The second time was slower

B. The second time was faster

C. The second time was harder

D. The second time was easier

Chapter 15 **The Second Miracle**

4. Where did Matilda go after she knocked over the glass a second time?

A. She went to the Trunchbull's office

B. She went to Miss Honey's house

C. She went flying past the stars on silver wings

D. She went home

Comprehension Quiz

1. Even though Matilda is excited about her new power, Miss Honey is still cautious. Why? (two answers)

A. Because Matilda might not be able to control her power

B. Miss Honey could be hurt by the power

C. Matilda could be hurt by overuse of her power

D. Matilda might lost her power

2. Miss Honey says that Matilda is a precocious child because_____.

A. Matilda is good at the magic power

B. Matilda is good at practical jokes

C. Matilda is good at math and reading

D. Matilda is out of control

Chapter 16 **Miss Honey's Cottage**

3. Miss Honey lives in a red brick cottage but Matilda thinks it looks like _____.

A. Hans Andersen's House

B. Ann's Green Gables

C. The Seven Dwarfs' house

D. Mickey Mouse's house

4. Where did Matilda find the water?

(A)_____

5. Is Miss Honey rich or poor?

(A) _____

Build your Vocabulary

13. The Weekly Test

- **assemble** [əsémbəl] *v.* 모으다, 조립하다
  To assemble something means to fit the different parts of it together.

- **utter** [ʌ́tər] ① *a.* 완전한, 전적인 ② *v.* (소리·말 등을) 입 밖에 내다, 발언하다
  Complete or extreme.

- **distaste** [distéist] *n.* (음식물에 대한) 싫음, 혐오
  A dislike of something which you find unpleasant or immoral.

- **nauseating** [nɔ́ːzièitiŋ] *a.* 욕지기나게 하는, 싫은
  Making you feel as if you are going to vomit.

- **wart** [wɔːrt] *n.* 사마귀
  A small hard lump which grows on the skin, often on the face and hands.

- **vomit** [vámit] *v.* 토하다, 게우다
  To empty the contents of the stomach through the mouth.

- **expel** [ikspél] *vt.* 쫓아내다, 물리치다
  To force to leave; to remove.

- **feed** [fiːd] (fed–fed) *vt.* (동물 등에) 먹이를 주다; 음식을 먹이다; 양육하다
  To give food to a person, group or animal.

- **bellow** [bélou] *vi.* 큰 소리로 울다; 고함지르다
  To shout in a loud voice, or (of a cow or large animal) to make a loud, deep sound.

- **blister** [blístər] *n.* (구어) 싫은 녀석; 물집, 수포; 부품; *v.* 물집이 생기다
  Some lazy bastard who always appears after the hard work has been finished.

- **filthy** [fílθi] *a.* 불결한, 더러운
  Extremely or unpleasantly dirty.

- **swell** [swel] *v.* 부풀다[게 하다], 붓다, 팽창하다 (up, out); 증가하다[시키다]
  To become larger and rounder than usual; to (cause to) increase in size or amount.

- **inflate** [infléit] *vt.* (공기·가스 등으로) 부풀게 하다, 부풀다
  To make something larger or more important.

- **jolly** [dʒáli] *a.* 명랑한, 즐거운, 유쾌한; *ad.* (영·구어) 대단히, 몹시
  Very.

Chapter 13-16

nasty [næsti] *a.* 더러운, 불쾌한, 몹시 싫은; 심술궂은, 험악한
Bad or very unpleasant.

peeve [pi:v] *v.* 애태우다, 안타깝게 하다, 성나게 하다
If you are peeved about something, you are annoyed about it.

pipe [paip] *v.* 피리를 불다; 지저귀다, 새된 목소리로 말하다; *n.* 파이프, 관
To speak or sing in a high voice.

wobble [wábəl] *v.* 흔들리다, 동요하다, 떨리다
To (cause something to) shake or move from side to side in a way that shows a lack of balance.

sarcasm [sá:rkæzəm] *n.* 빈정거림, 비꼼, 풍자
The use of remarks which clearly mean the opposite of what they say, and which are made in order to hurt someone's feelings or to criticize something in an amusing way.

diabolical [dàiəbálikəl] *a.* 악마의[같은], 마성의, 극악무도한
Extremely bad or shocking.

stalk [stɔ:k] *v.* (사냥감·사람 등에) 몰래 접근하다; 젠체하며 걷다, 활보하다
If you stalk somewhere, you walk there in a stiff, proud, or angry way.

ignorant [ígnərənt] *a.* 무지한, 예의를 모르는, (어떤 일을) 모르는
Not having enough knowledge, understanding or information about something.

slug [slʌg] *n.* 민달팽이
A small, usually black or brown, creature with a long soft body and no arms or legs, like a snail but with no shell.

witless [wítlis] *a.* 지혜[재치] 없는, 분별이 없는, 어리석은(foolish)
Stupid or lacking intelligence.

racquet [rǽkit] *n.* (=racket) 라켓 구기 (벽으로 둘러싸인 코트에서 함)
A net fixed tightly to an oval frame with a long handle, used in various sports for hitting a ball.

plait [pleit] *vt.* 닿다, 엮다, 접다, …에 주름잡다
To join three or more lengths of hair or string-like material by putting them over each other in a special pattern.

aloft [əlɔ́(:)ft] *ad.* 위에, 높이; [항해] 돛대 꼭대기에; (속어) 천국에
In the air or in a higher position.

Build your Vocabulary

squirm [skwə:rm] *vi.* (벌레처럼) 꿈틀거리다, 움직거리다, 꿈틀거리며 나아가다
To move from side to side in an awkward way because of nervousness, embarrassment or pain.

wriggle [rígəl] *v.* 꿈틀거리다, 몸부림치다; *n.* 몸부림침, 꿈틀거림
To twist your body, or move part of your body, with small, quick movements.

jerk [dʒə:rk] *v.* 갑자기 움직이다[당기다 · 밀치다]; *n.* 갑자기 잡아당김; 바보
To move or to make something move with a sudden short sharp movement.

gasp [gæsp] *v.* 헐떡거리다; 숨이 막히다; *n.* 헐떡거림, 숨막힘
To take a quick deep breath with your mouth open, especially because you are surprised or in pain.

whereupon [hwɛ̀ərəpán] *ad.* (관계사) 그래서, 그 때문에, 그 후에, 그 결과
Immediately after which.

plummet [plʌ́mit] *vi.* 수직으로 떨어지다; 뛰어들다; *n.* 낚싯봉, 가늠추
To fall very quickly and suddenly.

whimper [hwímpər] *vi.* 잦아들듯 울다; 훌쩍이다, 울먹이다
To make a series of small, weak sounds, expressing pain or unhappiness.

hypnotis[z]e [hípnətàiz] *v.* …에게 최면 걸다, 매혹하다, 무력화하다
To put someone in a state of hypnosis.

rivet [rívit] *vt.* 못 박다, 단단히 고정시키다
If you are riveted by something, it fascinates you and holds your interest completely.

infernal [infə́:rnl] *a.* 지옥의; 악마 같은
Very bad or unpleasant.

insolence [ínsələns] *n.* 오만, 무례; 오만한[건방진] 짓[말 · 태도]
Rude and not showing respect.

indelible [indéləbəl] *a.* 지울[씻을] 수 없는, 지워지지 않는, 잊혀지지 않는
Impossible to forget or remove.

pillar [pílər] *n.* 기둥, 대들보; 기둥 모양의 것
A strong column made of stone, metal or wood which supports part of a building.

doom [du:m] *n.* 운명, 파멸; *vt.* …의 운명을 정하다, 운명 짓다
Death, destruction or any very bad situation that cannot be avoided.

Chapter 13-16

- **squeal** [skwi:l] *v.* 꽥꽥거리다, 비명을 지르다
  If someone squeals, they make a long, high-pitched sound.

- **pedal** [pédl] *v.* 페달을 밟다
  To push the pedals of a bicycle round with your feet.

- **grimy** [gráimi] *a.* 때 묻은, 더러워진
  Something that is grimy is very dirty.

- **pixie** [píksi:] *n.* 작은 요정; 장난꾸러기; *a.* 장난치는, 장난기 있는
  A small imaginary person.

- **cope** [koup] *v.* 맞서다, 대처하다
  To deal successfully with a difficult situation.

- **brute** [bru:t] *n.* 짐승, 야만인; *a.* 잔인한, 야만적인, 금수와 같은, 무정한
  A rough and sometimes violent man.

- **birch** [bə:rtʃ] *n.* 자작나무로 만든 회초리
  An official punishment in the past, which involved hitting a person across the bottom with a stick, or the stick itself.

- **flick** [flik] *n.* (매·채찍 따위로) 찰싹[탁] 때리기; *v.* 찰싹[탁] 치다
  To move or hit something with a short sudden movement.

- **whopping** [hwápiŋ] *a.* (구어) 굉장한, 엄청난 (허풍 등); *ad.* 엄청나게, 굉장히
  If you describe an amount as whopping, you are emphasizing that it is large.

- **suicide** [sú:əsàid] *v.* 자살하다; *n.* 자살, 자해
  The act of killing yourself deliberately.

- **crook** [kruk] *n.* 갈고리; (구어) 사기꾼, 도둑; *v.* 구부리다; 훔치다
  If you crook your arm or finger, you bend it.

14. The First Miracle

- **bane** [bein] *n.* 파멸(의 원인); 맹독; 죽음; 재난
  A cause of continual trouble or unhappiness.

- **fly-spray** *n.* 파리 잡는 분무약

Build your Vocabulary

fly-paper *n.* 파리 잡이 끈끈이

porcelain [pɔ́:rsəlin] *a.* 자기로 만든, 깨지기 쉬운; *n.* 자기, (pl.) 자기 제품
A hard but delicate shiny white substance made by heating a special type of clay to a high temperature, used to make cups, plates, decorations, etc.

firecracker [fáiərkrækər] *n.* 폭죽, 딱총; 폭탄, 어뢰
A firework that makes a loud noise when it explodes.

squirm [skwə:rm] *vi.* (벌레처럼) 꿈틀거리다, 움직이다, 꿈틀거리며 나아가다
To move from side to side in an awkward way because of nervousness, embarrassment or pain.

quiver [kwívər] *vi.* 떨리다, 흔들리다
To shake slightly, often because of strong emotion.

blancmange [bləmá:ndʒ] *n.* 블라망주(우유로 만든 디저트의 일종)
A cold sweet food made from milk, sugar and cornflour.

wriggle [rígəl] *v.* 꿈틀거리다, 몸부림치다; *n.* 몸부림침, 꿈틀거림
To twist your body, or move part of your body, with small, quick movements.

fury [fjúəri] *n.* 격노, 격분; 격정, 열광, 광포, 격심함, 맹렬함
Extreme anger.

hatred [héitrid] *n.* 증오, 원한
An extremely strong feeling of dislike.

smoulder [smóuldər] *v.* 그을려서 검게 하다, 그을다, 연기 피우다
To burn slowly with smoke but without flames.

maggot [mǽgət] *n.* 구더기
A creature like a very small worm which later develops into a fly and is found in decaying meat and other foods.

reluctantly [rilʌ́ktəntli] *ad.* 마지못해, 싫어하면서
Not very willing to do something and therefore slow to do it.

vile [vail] *a.* 비열한, 야비한
If you say that someone or something is vile, you mean that they are very unpleasant.

repulsive [ripʌ́lsiv] *a.* 되쫓아버리는, 박차는; 쌀쌀한; 싫은, 불쾌한
To causes someone to have a strong feeling of dislike, disapproval or disgust.

Chapter 13-16

repellent [ripélənt] *a.* (사람에게) 혐오감을 주는, 불쾌한, 쌀쌀한, 쫓아버리는
Very unpleasant; causing strong dislike.

malicious [məlíʃəs] *a.* 악의 있는, 심술궂은; 고의의, 부당한
Intended to harm or upset other people.

drum out *phrasal v.* ① …을 추방[제명]하다(of) ② (북을 두드려 메시지)를 보내다
To force someone to leave a job, group, etc., often because they have behaved in a way which is not considered honourable.

disgrace [disgréis] *n.* 불명예, 치욕, 창피
Embarrassment and the loss of other people's respect, or behaviour which causes this.

reformatory [rifɔ́:rmətɔ̀:ri] *n.* 소년원
A boarding school where young people could be sent to stay if they had been found guilty of a crime.

delinquent [dilíkwənt] *n.* 태만한 사람, 범법자, 비행 소년; *a.* 직무 태만의
A person, usually young, who behaves in a way that is illegal or unacceptable to most people.

fleck [flek] *n.* 반점, 얼룩, 주근깨
A small mark or spot.

froth [frɔ:θ] *n.* 거품 *v.* 거품을 일으키다
To have or produce a lot of small bubbles which often rise to the surface.

accuse [əkjú:z] *v.* 비난하다, 고발하다
To charge (someone) with having done something wrong.

roar [rɔ:r] *vi.* 으르렁거리다, 고함치다, 외치다
To make a long, loud, deep sound.

pin ... on a person *idiom* (구어) …에게 …의 책임을 지우다
If someone tries to pin something on you, they say, often unfairly, that you were responsible for something bad or illegal.

rant [rænt] *v.* 폭언하다, 고함치다, 호통치다
To speak or complain about something in a loud and/or angry way.

maniac [méiniæk] *a.* 광적인, 광란의; *n.* (구어) 열광자, 마니아
A person who has a very strong interest in a particular activity.

Build your Vocabulary

- **expel** [ikspél] *vt.* 쫓아내다, 물리치다
  To force to leave; to remove.

- **march up** *phrasal v.* 출세 가도를 달리다

- **tremble** [trémbəl] *v.* 떨다, 떨리다
  To shake slightly, usually because you are cold or frightened.

- **rivet** [rívit] *vt.* 못 박다, 단단히 고정시키다
  To fasten together with a rivet.

- **creep** [kri:p] (crept-crept) *vi.* 기다, 살금살금 걷다
  To move slowly, quietly and carefully, usually in order to avoid being noticed.

- **peculiar** [pikjú:ljər] *a.* 기묘한, 이상한; 특이한, 눈에 띄는
  Unusual and strange, sometimes in an unpleasant way.

- **brew** [bru:] *vt.* 양조하다, (혼합 음료를) 만들다
  If you brew tea or coffee, you add boiling water to it to make a hot drink, and if it brews, it gradually develops flavour in the container in which it was made.

- **tip** [tip] *v.* 기울이다, 뒤집어엎다
  To (cause to) move so that one side is higher than another side.

- **wobble** [wábəl] *v.* 흔들리다, 동요하다, 떨리다
  To (cause something to) shake or move from side to side in a way that shows a lack of balance.

- **fraction** [frǽkʃən] *n.* 파편, 단편; 조금, 소량; [수학] 분수
  A fraction of something is a tiny amount or proportion of it.

- **teeter** [tí:tər] *v.* 흔들리다, 비틀거리며 나가다
  To appear to be about to fall while moving or standing.

- **topple** [tápəl] *vi.* 넘어지다, 쓰러지다
  To (cause to) lose balance and fall down.

- **tinkle** [tíŋkəl] *v.* 딸랑딸랑 울리다
  A light ringing sound.

- **bosom** [búzəm] *n.* (문어) 가슴, 흉부; 가슴속(의 생각), 내심; 속, 내부
  A woman's breasts.

Chapter 13-16

CJ 복습 **clutch** [klʌtʃ] *v.t.* 꽉 잡다, 붙들다
To take or try to take hold of something tightly.

swipe [swaip] *v.* 강타하다; (구어) 들치기하다, 훔치다; *n.* 강타, 맹타; 비난, 비평
To hit or try to hit something, especially with a sideways movement.

⁎ **duck** [dʌk] ① *n.* 오리; ② *v.* 물속으로 들어가다; 피하다, 회피하다
To move your head or the top part of your body quickly down to avoid being hit.

⁎ **serenity** [sərénəti] *n.* 고요함, 맑음, 화창함, 청명
Peaceful and calm; troubled by nothing.

⁎ **soak** [souk] *v.* 적시다, 젖다; 푹 젖게 하다; 스며들다[나오다]
To put something in liquid for a time so that it becomes completely wet.

⁎⁎ **compel** [kəmpél] *v.t.* 강제하다, 억지로 …시키다
To force someone to do something.

복습 **clot** [klɑt] *n.* (엉긴) 덩어리, 떼; *v.* 덩어리지다, 응고하다
An almost solid lump.

복습 **carbuncle** [káːrbʌŋkəl] *n.* [의학] 등창; 여드름, 뽀루지; [광물] 홍옥(紅玉)
A large painful swelling under the skin.

복습 **infuriate** [infjúərièit] *v.t.* 격노케 하다
To make someone extremely angry.

⁎ **vouch** [vautʃ] *v.* 보증하다, 증인이 되다, 단언하다, 입증하다
To be able from your knowledge or experience to say that something is true.

flinch [flintʃ] *v.i.* 주춤하다, 움찔하다
To make a sudden small movement because of pain or fear.

be fed up with *idiom* (구어) …에 물리다, 싫증나다
If you are fed up, you are unhappy, bored, or tired of something, especially something that you have been experiencing for a long time.

CJ **midget** [mídʒit] *n.* 난쟁이, 꼬마; 초소형의 것; *a.* 보통보다 작은, 극소형의
A very small person.

복습 **stun** [stʌn] *v.t.* 어리벙벙하게 하다, 기절시키다
To shock or surprise someone very much.

Build your Vocabulary

15. The Second Miracle

astound [əstáund] *v.* 깜짝 놀라게 하다, 몹시 놀라게 하다
If something astounds you, you are very surprised by it.

spur [spəːr] *n.* 박차, 자극; *v.* 박차를 가하다
To encourage an activity or development or make it happen faster.

confide [kənfáid] *v.* 털어놓다, 신뢰하다
To tell something secret or personal to someone whom you trust not to tell anyone else.

riffle [rifəl] *v.* 펄럭펄럭 넘기다; *n.* 급류; 잔물결; 펄럭펄럭 넘기는 것
To look quickly through the pages of a book, magazine, etc., or through a collection of things.

peculiar [pikjúːljər] *a.* 기묘한, 이상한; 특이한, 눈에 띄는
Unusual and strange, sometimes in an unpleasant way.

alert [əláːrt] *v.* 경고하다, 경계시키다; *a.* 방심하지 않는; *n.* 경보, 경계
To warn someone of a possibly dangerous situation.

disastrous [dizǽstrəs] *a.* 비참한, 피해가 막심한; (고어) 불길한, 불운한
Great harm, damage or death, or serious difficulty.

exalt [igzɔ́ːlt] *v.* 높이다, 올리다, 칭찬하다, 찬양하다, 몹시 기쁘게 하다
To praise someone a lot.

expel [ikspel] *v.* 내쫓다, 쫓아버리다; 추방하다, 제명하다
To officially make somebody leave a school or an organization.

topple [tápəl] *vi.* 넘어지다, 쓰러지다
To (cause to) lose balance and fall down.

rim [rim] *n.* (둥근 물건의) 가장자리, 테두리, 테; *v.* 둘러싸다, 테를 두르다
To form an edge around something.

spectacle [spektəkəl] *n.* 광경, 장관; (pl.) 안경
An unusual or unexpected event or situation which attracts attention, interest or disapproval.

willed [wild] *a.* …의 의지가 있는
Having a strong will.

Chapter 13-16

- **vivid** [vívid] *a.* 생생한, 발랄한
  Produce very clear, powerful and detailed images in the mind.

- **cup** [kʌp] *n.* 한 잔; *vt.* 잔에 넣다, (손 등을) 잔 모양으로 만들다[하여 받치다]
  If you cup something in your hands, you make your hands into a curved dish-like shape and support it or hold it gently.

- **surge** [sə:rdʒ] *n.* 큰 물결, 쇄도; *v.* 파도처럼 밀려오다
  A sudden quick movement of electricity through something.

- **strike** [straik] (struck-struck) *v.* 치다, 찌르다; 충돌하다; 인상을 남기다
  (of a thought or an idea) To come into somebody's mind suddenly.

- **dumb** [dʌm] *a.* 벙어리의, 말을 못 하는, 말을 하지 않는
  Permanently or temporarily unable to speak.

- **seraphic** [səræfik] *a.* 천사의[같은]; 거룩한; 맑은
  As beautiful, pure, etc. as an angel.

- **awestruck** [ɔ́:strʌ̀k] *a.* 위엄에 눌린, 위압당한
  Filled with feelings of admiration or respect.

- **cottage** [kátidʒ] *n.* 오두막집, 시골집
  A small house, usually in the countryside.

16. Miss Honey's Cottage

- **animate** [ǽnəmèit] *vt.* 살리다, 활기를 주다; *a.* 살아 있는, 활기 있는
  To make someone seem more happy or active.

- **valve** [vælv] *n.* (장치의) 판(瓣), 밸브
  A device which opens and closes to control the flow of liquids or gases, or a similar structure in the heart and the veins, which controls the flow of blood.

- **trot** [trɑt] *v.* 속보로 걷다, 빨리 걷다; 총총걸음 치다
  To move fairly fast at a speed between walking and running, taking small quick steps.

- **tread** [tred] *n.* 발판, 페달; *v.* 밟다, 걷다
  The part of a wheel that comes into contact with a rail, the ground.

- **divine** [diváin] *a.* 신의, 신성한; 신묘한, 비범한
  Connected with a god, or like a god.

Build your Vocabulary

steam up *idiom* ① 흐려지다 ② 기운을 내다; 흥분시키다 ③ (술에) 취하다

phenomenon [finámənàn] *n.* 현상
A fact or an event in nature or society, especially one that is not fully understood.

bowl over *idiom* (구어) …을 때려눕히다; …을 몹시 놀래다, 당황하게 하다
To knock someone to the ground by running into them.

precocious [prikóuʃəs] *a.* (아이·거동 따위) 조숙한, 일된, 어른다운
Describes a child who behaves as if they are much older than they are.

conceit [kənsíːt] *n.* 자부심, 자만
When you are too proud of yourself and your actions.

glimmer [glímər] *vi.* 희미하게 빛나다; 깜빡이다
To shine with a weak light or a light that is not continuous.

hawthorn [hɔ́ːθɔːrn] *n.* [식물] 산사나무 속(屬) (특히 서양산사나무)
A type of small wild tree with thorns, white or pink flowers in spring and small red fruits in the autumn.

sycamore [síkəmɔ̀ːr] *n.* 단풍나무의 일종; [미국] 플라타너스(buttonwood)
A tree with leaves divided into five parts and seeds that spin slowly to the ground when they fall.

chestnut [tʃésnʌt] *n.* 밤, 밤나무
A large shiny reddish-brown nut, or the tree on which the nuts grow.

barred [bɑːrd] *a.* 빗장을 지른; 가로 줄무늬가 있는
If someone is barred from a place or from doing something, they are officially forbidden to go there or to do it.

rut [rʌt] *vt.* 바퀴 자국을 내다, 홈을 내다; *n.* 바퀴 자국, 홈
A deep narrow mark made in soft ground especially by a wheel.

hedge [hedʒ] *n.* (산)울타리; 경계; *v.* 산울타리를 만들다; 제한하다; 여지를 남기다
A way of protecting, controlling or limiting something.

hazel [héizəl] *n., a.* 개암(나무)(의); 담갈색(의)
A small tree that produces nuts that can be eaten.

cluster [klʌ́stər] *v.* 집중 발생하다; 밀집하다[시키다]; 떼 짓다[짓게 하다]
If people cluster together, they gather together in a small group.

Chapter 13-16

ripe [raip] *a.* 익은, 여문
Completely developed and ready to be collected or eaten.

bleak [bli:k] *a.* 황폐한, 삭막한, 쓸쓸한
Cold, empty, and unattractive.

dwell [dwel] *vi.* 살다, 거주하다, 머무르다
To live in a place or in a particular way.

crumbly [krʌ́mbli] *a.* 부서지기 쉬운, 푸석푸석한
Breaking easily into small pieces.

chimney [tʃímni] *n.* 굴뚝
A hollow structure that allows the smoke from a fire inside a building to escape to the air outside.

nettle [nétl] *n.* [식물] 쐐기풀
A wild plant with heart-shaped leaves that are covered in hairs which sting.

thorn [θɔ:rn] *n.* (식물의) 가시
A small sharp pointed growth on the stem of a plant.

hearthstone [há:rθstòun] *n.* 노[용광로]의 바닥 돌; 광내는 돌

blithe [blaið] *a.* 즐거운, 유쾌한, 쾌활한; 경솔한, 부주의한
Happy and without worry.

flock [flɑk] *n.* 무리, 떼; *vi.* 무리 짓다, 모이다
A group of sheep, goats or birds, or a group of people.

dew [dju:] *n.* 이슬; (시어) 신선함, 상쾌함; *v.* 이슬로 적시다[젖다]; 축이다
Drops of water that form on the ground and other surfaces outside during the night.

profound [prəfáund] *a.* 깊이가 있는, 심오한
Felt or experienced very strongly or in an extreme way.

flaky [fléiki] *a.* 벗겨지기 쉬운; 조각조각의; (미·속어) 색다른, 별난
If you describe an idea, argument, or person as flaky, you mean that they are rather eccentric and unreliable.

stoop [stu:p] *vi.* (몸을) 구부리다, 굴복하다
To bend the top half of the body forward and down.

Build your Vocabulary

Primus [práiməs] *n.* 프라이머스 (휴대용 석유 난로; 상표명)

paraffin [pǽrəfin] *n.* [화학] 파라핀
A clear liquid with a strong smell made from coal or petroleum and used as a fuel, especially in heaters and lights.

bemused [bimjú:zd] *a.* 생각에 잠긴; 멍한, 어리벙벙한; 곤혹스러운, 망연한
Slightly confused.

c ★ **dangle** [dǽŋɡəl] *v.* 매달다[리다]; 따라다니다; *n.* 매달린 것
To hang loosely, or to hold something so that it hangs loosely.

★ **slack** [slæk] *a.* (로프·새끼 등이) 늘어진, 느슨한; 되는대로의; 꾸물거리는
Not stretched tight.

lo and behold *idiom* 보라, 자 보시라; 이게 어찌된 영문인가!
(humorous)Used for calling attention to a surprising or annoying thing.

복습 ★ **bare** [bɛər] *a.* 발가벗은, 헐벗은; 빈, 텅 빈; 가까스로의
A bare surface is not covered or decorated with anything.

★ **delicacy** [délikəsi] *n.* 민감, 예민함, 미묘함, 섬세함, 우아함
Pleasantly soft or light; not strong.

복습 **plank** [plæŋk] *n.* 널, 두꺼운 판자
A long narrow flat piece of wood or similar material, of the type used for making floors.

J **grime** [graim] *n.* 때, 먼지, 검댕
A layer of dirt on skin or on a building.

복습 **palm** [pɑ:m] *n.* 손바닥
The palm of your hand is the inside part.

복습 **appall** [əpɔ́:l] *vt.* 오싹 소름이 끼치게 하다, 섬뜩하게 하다
To make someone have strong feelings of shock or of disapproval.

복습 **neat** [ni:t] *a.* 산뜻한, 깔끔한 (neatly *ad.* 깔끔하게)
Tidy, with everything in its place.

★ **trim** [trim] *v.* 다듬다, 정돈하다, 손질하다; 잘라내다, 없애다
To make something tidier or more level by cutting a small amount off it.

Chapter 13-16

- ✽ **perch** [pəːrtʃ] *v.* 앉다, 자리를 차지하다, (높은 곳에) 놓다, 앉히다
  To sit on or near the edge of something.

- ✽ **compel** [kəmpél] *v.t.* 강제하다, 억지로 …시키다
  To force someone to do something.

- ✽ **fasciate** [fǽʃièit] *v.* 매혹하다, 반하게 하다; 주의를 끌다
  If something fascinates you, it interests and delights you so much that your thoughts tend to concentrate on it.

Crossword Puzzle

Use the clues and the words in the box to complete the crossword puzzle.

ignorant   froth   astound   infuriate   spur   teeter   appall   duck
crook   compel   conceit   blithe   cluster   crumbly   tremble   wriggle
fraction   topple   peculiar   assembler

Chapter 13-16

Across

3   Not having enough knowledge, understanding or information about something.
5   To have or produce a lot of small bubbles which often rise to the surface.
7   Breaking easily into small pieces.
8   To be very surprised by something.
10 When you are too proud of yourself and your actions.
12 If you _____ your arm or finger, you bend it.
15 To encourage an activity or development or make it happen faster.
16 To make someone extremely angry.
17 Happy and without worry.
18 To fit the different parts of something together.
19 To (cause to) lose balance and fall down.

Down

1   Unusual and strange, sometimes in an unpleasant way.
2   A tiny amount or proportion of something.
4   To make someone have strong feelings of shock or of disapproval.
6   If people _____ together, they gather together in a small group.
9   To move your head or the top part of your body quickly down, especially to avoid being hit.
11 To appear to be about to fall while moving or standing.
12 To force someone to do something.
13 To twist your body, or move part of your body, with small, quick movements.
14 To shake slightly, usually because you are cold or frightened

Comprehension Quiz

1. Put these tragedies in Miss Honey's life in order.
(- - -)
A. Her parents died
B. She had to be a slave for her Aunt
C. She had to pay back all of her debts to her Aunt
D. She was beaten by her Aunt

2. How long has Miss Honey been free from her Aunt?
(A)_____

3. Why does Miss Honey only get one pound per week salary?
(A)_____

4. What is not the reason Miss Honey doesn't get help?
A. She doesn't have enough money
B. She is too afraid of her aunt
C. She doesn't have any other family in England who can help her
D. She doesn't need any help

Chapter 17 **Miss Honey's Story**

5. How can the Aunt keep the house instead of the daughter?

A. She is closer blood relation

B. She is meaner

C. She has a paper from the dead father naming her as the owner of the house

D. She took care of Miss Honey so the aunt should get the house as payment

* **chapter 18. The Names (No Questions)**

Comprehension Quiz

1. When Matilda practiced her eye power what did she use?

A. A brush

B. A mirror

C. A cigar

D. A book

2. Was it easy or hard to learn to lift the cigar?

(A)_____

3. what did Matilda whisper in practice? [two answers]

A. "Tip!"

B. "Move!"

C. "Fall!"

D. "Lift!"

4. Mark the following statements either True(T) or False(F).

A. When Matilda had a practice, her parents came back to the house ( )

B. Matilda had enjoyed the practice ( )

C. In the end, Matilda could lift the cigar into the air ( )

Chapter 19 **The Practice**

5. How long did she practice until she was ready?

A. For two days

B. For six days

C. For a week

D. For a month

Comprehension Quiz

1. What are the students supposed to know for today's test with Miss Trunchbull?

A. How to spell wrong backwards

B. The three times tables

C. How to do adding up

D. How to play with a newt

2. Whose message did Matilda write on the board with her eyes?

A. Miss Honey's

B. The Trunchbul's

C. Miss Honey's father's

D. Mr. Wormwood's

Chapter 20 **The Third Miracle**

3. Put the following events in order. (-   -   -   )

A. Miss Trunchbull fainted

B. Miss Trunchbull disappeared forever

C. Nigel poured water on Miss Trunchbull's face

D. Teachers came to carry her away

> Agatha, give my Jenny back her house

> Give my Jenny her wages
> Give my Jenny the house
> Then get out of here.
> If you don't, I will come and get you
> I will come and get you like you got me.
> I am watching you Agatha—.

Comprehension Quiz

1. Who became the new head master of the school?

(A)_____

2. What class did Matilda study in?

(A)_____

3. Why did Matilda's magic powers disappear?

A. She was bored

B. The Trunchbull was gone

C. She was using her mental power to learn in an exciting class

D. She was getting older

Chapter 21 **A New Home**

4. Put the events in order. (　-　-　-　)

A. Miss Honey moves into her father's house

B. Miss Honey adopts Matilda

C. Miss Honey has tea with Matilda

D. Miss Honey gets a letter about her father's money

5. Why does Matilda's family have to move to Spain? (two answers)

A. Because they have been selling cars with three wheels

B. Because they have no more money

C. Because the police are chasing the Wormwoods

D. Because the Wormwoods have been selling stolen cars

6. What happened to Matilda and Miss Honey?

A. Matilda left Miss Honey

B. They lived happily ever after

C. Miss Honey didn't have time to play with Matilda anymore

D. They lived in different areas but met each other from time to time

Build your Vocabulary

17. Miss Honey's Story

* **stiff** [stif] *a.* 굳은, 뻣뻣한; 완강한, 완고한 (stiffly *ad.* 완고하게, 뻣뻣하게)
  More difficult or sever than usual.

* **ornament** [ɔ́:rnəmənt] *n.* 꾸밈, 장식; *vt.* 꾸미다, 장식하다
  To add decoration to something.

  fridge [fridʒ] *n.* (=refrigerator) (구어) 냉장고
  A piece of kitchen equipment which uses electricity to preserve food at a cold temperature.

* **rigid** [rídʒid] *a.* 굳은, 단단한; 엄격한, 완고한
  Stiff or fixed; not able to be bent, moved, changed or persuaded.

c * **hunch** [hʌntʃ] *n.* 군살, 혹; (구어) 예감, 육감; *vt.* (등을) 둥글게 구부리다
  To lean forward with your shoulders raised or to bend your back and shoulders into a rounded shape.

* **rouse** [rauz] *vt.* 깨우다, 눈뜨게 하다; 환기하다, 고무하다; *n.* 각성
  To wake someone up or make someone more active or excited.

* **stare** [stɛər] *v.* 응시하다, 빤히 보다, 노려보다; *n.* 응시
  To look at somebody/something for a long time.

* **awkward** [ɔ́:kwərd] *a.* 어색한, 서투른; 힘든 (awkwardness *n.* 어색함, 거북함)
  Making you feel embarrassed.

c **stagger** [stǽgər] *v.* 비틀거리다[게 하다]; 흔들리다[게 하다]
  To walk or move with a lack of balance as if you are going to fall.

J * **tuck** [tʌk] *v.* 밀어 넣다, 쑤셔 넣다
  To put or fold something into a small space.

* **tragedy** [trǽdʒədi] *n.* 비극, 비극적인 이야기
  A very sad event or situation, especially one involving death or suffering, or a play or literature about death or suffering.

J * **sip** [sip] *n.* 한 모금; *vt.* 찔끔찔끔 마시다
  A very small amount of a drink.

c * **shrug** [ʃrʌg] *v.* (어깨를) 으쓱하다
  To raise up and drop the shoulders briefly as an indication of doubt, indifference, etc.

granny [grǽni] *n.* (구어·유아어) 할머니; 노파
Grandmother.

cow [kau] ① *n.* 암소 ② *vt.* 으르다, 위협하다
If someone is cowed, they are made afraid, or made to behave in a particular way because they have been frightened.

gut [gʌt] *n.* 창자, 내장; 직감, 본능, 신경; (pl.) 용기, 결단; 실질, 핵심
Guts is the will and courage to do something which is difficult or unpleasant.

petrify [pètrəfài] *v.* 돌이 되게 하다, 돌같이 굳게 하다, 깜짝 놀라게 하다
To frighten someone greatly, especially so that they are unable to move or speak.

pluck up *idiom* 힘[용기]을 내다, 분발하다; 근절시키다, 뽑아버리다
To force yourself to be brave enough to do something, although you are frightened or anxious about it.

steel [sti:l] *n.* 강철; *vt.* 강철을 입히다, 견고하게 하다; (마음을) 단단히 하다
If you steel yourself, you prepare to deal with something unpleasant.

possess [pəzés] *vt.* 소유하다, 가지고 있다
To have or own something, or to have a particular quality.

mumble [mʌ́mbəl] *v.* 중얼거리다, 웅얼거리다; 우물우물 씹다; *n.* 중얼거림
To speak unclearly and quietly so that the words are difficult to understand.

marvellous [má:rvələs] (=marvelous) *a.* 놀라운, 믿기 어려운
Extremely good.

clarity [klǽrəti] *n.* (사상·문제 등의) 명쾌함, 명석함
The quality of being clear and easy to understand.

kin [kin] *n.* 친척, 친족 (next of kin : 가장 가까운 친족)
Family and relatives.

forgery [fɔ́:rdʒəri] *n.* (문서·화폐 따위의) 위조, 위조죄, 위조품[문서], 위폐
To make an illegal copy of something in order to deceive.

18. The Names

snip [snip] *vt.* (가위로) 자르다, 싹둑 베다; *n.* 싹둑 자름, 가위질
To cut something with scissors, usually with small quick cuts.

Build your Vocabulary

authority [əθɔ́:riti] *n.* 권위, 권력, 위신
The power or right to control or judge others, or to have the final say in something.

ponder [pándər] *v.* 숙고하다, 깊이 생각하다
To think carefully about something, especially for a noticeable length of time.

19. The Practice

ethereal [iθíriəl] *a.* 가뿐한, 공기 같은, 천상의, 하늘의
Light and delicate, especially in an unnatural way.

vital [váitl] *a.* 생명의, 생생한; 중요한, 치명적인
Necessary for the success or continued existence of something; extremely important.

summon [sʌ́mən] *v.* 소환하다, 호출하다
To order someone to come to or be present at a particular place, or to officially arrange a meeting of people.

trigger [trígər] *n.* (총의) 방아쇠; 계기, 자극
A part of a gun which causes the gun to fire when pressed.

fiercely [fiərsli] *ad.* 맹렬히, 지독히
In a frightening, violent or powerful way.

colossal [kəlásəl] *a.* 거대한, 어마어마한; (구어) 훌륭한, 놀랄 만한
Extremely large.

sheer [ʃiər] *a.* 얇은, 순전한, 섞이지 않은; 깎아지른 듯한; *ad.* 완전히, 순전히
Used to emphasize how very great, important or powerful a quality or feeling is.

20. The Third Miracle

jolly [dʒáli] *a.* 명랑한, 즐거운, 유쾌한; *ad.* (영·구어) 대단히, 몹시
Very.

smart alec(k) *n.* (구어) 건방진 놈; 잘난[똑똑한] 체하는 놈
Someone who tries to appear clever or who answers questions in a clever way that annoys other people.

cheeky [tʃí:ki] *a.* (구어) 건방진, 뻔뻔스러운
Rudeness or lack of respect.

Chapter 17-21

reassemble [rìːəsémbəl] *v.* 다시 모으다[모이다]; 새로 짜 맞추다
If a group of people reassembles or if you reassemble them, they gather together again in a group.

apprehensive [æ̀prihénsiv] *a.* 우려하는, 염려하는; 이해가 빠른, 총명한 (apprehensively *ad.* 염려하여, 총명하게)
Anxiety about the future or a fear that something unpleasant is going to happen.

tigress [táigris] *n.* 암컷 호랑이; 잔인한 여자
A woman who is behaving very fiercely.

venture [véntʃər] *v.* 위험을 무릅쓰고 하다, 감히 …하다
To risk going somewhere or doing something that might be dangerous or unpleasant, or to risk saying something that might be criticized.

impertinent [impə́ːrtənənt] *a.* 건방진, 뻔뻔한; 적절하지 않은, 관계없는
Rude and not showing respect for somebody who is older or more important.

blither [blíðər] *vi.* 허튼 소리를 하다
An extremely stupid person.

fester [féstər] *v.* (상처가) 곪다, 곪게 하다; 괴롭히다, 괴로워하다
If a cut or other injury festers, it becomes infected and produces pus.

gumboil [gʌ́mbɔ̀il] *n.* 잇몸 궤양

fleabitten [flíːbàitn] *a.* 벼룩에 물린; 흰 바탕에 갈색 반점이 있는; 지저분한
Dirty and in bad condition.

fungus [fʌ́ŋgəs] *n.* 버섯, 균류
Any of various types of organism which obtain their food from decaying material or other living things.

stagnant [stǽgnənt] *a.* 흐르지 않는, 괴어 있는, 정체된; 불경기의, 부진한
Not flowing or moving, and smelling unpleasant.

cesspool [séspùːl] *n.* 구정물 구덩이, 시궁창, 분뇨 구덩이; (비유) 불결한 장소
A large underground hole or container which is used for collecting and storing excrement, urine and dirty water.

fluster [flʌ́stər] *v.* 당황하다, 혼란스럽게 하다
If you fluster someone, you make them upset and confused.

Build your Vocabulary

blister [blístər] *n.* (구어) 싫은 녀석; 물집, 수포; 부품; *v.* 물집이 생기다
Some lazy bastard who always appears after the hard work has been finished.

maggot [mǽgət] *n.* 구더기
A creature like a very small worm which later develops into a fly and is found in decaying meat and other foods.

mangle [mǽŋgəl] *vt.* 난도질하다, 엉망으로 만들다
To destroy something by twisting or tearing it that its original form is changed.

wurzel *n.* (영) [식물] 비트(beet) (가축 사료)

look sharp *idiom* (명령형으로) 서둘러라, 빨리 해라, 마음놓지 마라

bewilder [biwíldər] *vt.* 당황하게 하다, 어리둥절하게 하다
If something bewilders you, it is so confusing that you cannot understand it.

gymnastic [dʒimnǽstik] *a.* 체조[체육]의, (지적·육체적) 단련[노력]을 요하는
Physical exercises that develop and show the body°Øs strength and ability to move and bend easily, often done as a sport in competitions.

judo [dʒúːdou] *n.* 유도
A sport in which two people fight using their arms and legs and hands and feet, and try to throw each other to the ground.

karate [kǽrət] *n.* 가라테 (태권도 비슷한 일본의 호신술)
A Japanese system of fighting in which you use your hands and feet as weapons.

somersault [sʌ́mərsɔ̀ːlt] *n.* 재주넘기, 공중제비
A rolling movement or jump, either forwards or backwards, in which you turn over completely, with your body above your head, and finish with your head on top again.

pluck [plʌk] *v.* 잡아 뜯다, 잡아당기다
To pull something, especially with a sudden movement, in order to remove it.

shrill [ʃril] *a.* (소리가) 날카로운, 새된, 높은
Having a loud and high sound that is unpleasant or painful to listen to.

hover [hʌ́vər] *v.* 하늘을 떠다니다, 비상하다
To stay in one place in the air.

compress [kəmprés] *v.* 압축하다[되다]; 요약하다, 집약하다
To press something into a smaller space.

c **halibut** [hæləbət] *n.* [어류] 북방 해양 산의 큰 넙치, 핼리벗
A big, flat sea fish which can be eaten.

✱ **strangle** [stræŋgəl] *vt.* 교살하다, 질식(사)시키다
To kill someone by pressing their throat so that they cannot breathe.

✱ **tinkle** [tíŋkəl] *v.* 딸랑딸랑 울리다
A light ringing sound.

✸ **kneel** [niːl] *vi.* (knelt-knelt) 무릎 꿇다
To lower oneself onto one's knees.

✱ **prostrate** [prástreit] *a.* 엎어진, 엎드린, 항복한, 패배한
Lying with the face down and arms stretched out, especially in obedience or worship.

✸ **fetch** [fetʃ] *vt.* (가서) 가져오다, 데려오다, 불러오다
To go to another place to get something or someone and bring them back.

✱ **matron** [méitrən] *n.* 양호 선생님; 여사, 가정부, 보모
A women who works as a nurse in a school.

c ✸ **seize** [siːz] *vt.* 붙잡다
If you seize something, you take hold of it quickly, firmly, and forcefully.

elate [iléit] *vt.* 기운을 돋우다, 의기양양하게 하다
Extremely happy and excited, often because something has happened or been achieved.

✸ **scorch** [skɔːrtʃ] *v.* 태우다, 그슬리다
To change colour with dry heat, or to burn slightly.

21. A New Home

✱ **enquire** [inkwáiər] (=inquire) *v.* 묻다, 문의하다
To ask for information.

bunk [bʌŋk] *n.* 도망 (do a bunk : 도망가다, 내빼다)
To leave suddenly and unexpectedly.

J ✸ **vanish** [vǽniʃ] *v.* 사라지다, 자취를 감추다
To disappear suddenly.

Build your Vocabulary

- **solicitor** [səlísətər] *n.* 간청자, 권유자; 사무 변호사, 법무관
  A type of lawyer in Britain and Australia who is trained to prepare cases and give advice on legal subjects and can represent people in lower courts.

- **testament** [téstəmənt] *n.* 유언(장), 유서
  (보통 유언은 one's last will and testament라고 씀)
  Someone's last will and testament is the most recent will that they have made, especially the last will that they make before they die.

- **perch** [pəːrtʃ] *v.* 앉다, 자리를 차지하다, (높은 곳에) 놓다, 앉히다
  To sit on or near the edge of something.

- **hedgehog** [hédʒhàg] *n.* ① 고슴도치 ② 견고한 요새 ③ 성 잘 내는 심술쟁이
  A small brown animal with sharp spikes covering its back.

- **journey** [dʒə́ːrni] *n.* 여행
  The act of travelling from one place to another, especially in a vehicle.

- **confront** [kənfránt] *vt.* 직면하다, 마주 대하다; 대조하다
  To face, meet or deal with a difficult situation or person.

- **gravel** [grǽvəl] *n.* 자갈; *vt.* 자갈로 덮다, …에 자갈을 깔다
  Small rounded stones, often mixed with sand.

- **crimson** [krímzən] *a.* 진홍색의; *n.* 진홍색
  Having a dark deep red colour.

- **crook** [kruk] *n.* 갈고리; (구어) 사기꾼, 도둑; *v.* 구부리다; 훔치다
  If you crook your arm or finger, you bend it.

- **tip off** *idiom* 비밀 정보를 누설하다, 밀고하다; …에게 (위험·재난 등을) 경고하다
  A tip-off is a piece of information or a warning that you give to someone, often privately or secretly.

- **tuppence** [tʌ́pəns] *n.* (영) 2펜스(TWOPENCE), 시시한 일
  (do not care tuppence(twopence) : 조금도 상관[개의]치 않다)
  To not care about something or someone in any way.

- **scurry** [skə́ːri] *vi.* 급히 가다, 종종걸음으로 달리다
  When people or small animals scurry somewhere, they move there quickly and hurriedly, especially because they are frightened.

Chapter 17-21

burst out *idiom* 튀어 나오다; 갑자기 나타나다[…하기 시작하다 · 소리 지르다]
To suddenly say something loudly.

stow [stou] *v.t.* (짐을) 실어 넣다, (물건을) 싣다, 집어넣다
To store something.

consent [kənsént] *v.i.* 동의하다, 승낙하다; *n.* 동의, 승낙
Permission or agreement.

tyre [taiər] (=tire) (고무로 만든) 타이어
A thick rubber ring, often filled with air, which is fitted around the outer edge of the wheel of a vehicle, allowing the vehicle to stick to the road surface and to travel over the ground more easily.

tear round *idiom* (구어) (흥분 · 분노하여) 법석을 떨며 돌아다니다

Crossword Puzzle

Use the clues and the words in the box to complete the crossword puzzle.

ponder, pluck, mumble, fluster, stiff, stare, venture, compress, stagger, authority, fiercely, seize, tragedy, sip, bewilder, consent, kneel, vanish, confront, scurry, scorch, reassemble

Chapter 17-21

Across

3 To think carefully about something, especially for a noticeable length of time.
6 To speak unclearly and quietly so that the words are difficult to understand.
7 To change colour with dry heat, or to burn slightly.
12 If you _____ someone, you make them upset and confused.
14 Permission or agreement.
17 A very small amount of a drink.
19 A very sad event or situation, especially one involving death or suffering, or a play or literature about death or suffering.
20 To face, meet or deal with a difficult situation or person.
21 In a frightening, violent or powerful way.

Down

1 To take hold of something quickly, firmly, and forcefully.
2 To come together again, or bring something together again, in a single place.
4 To look at somebody/something for a long time.
5 The power or right to control or judge others, or to have the final say in something.
7 To move quickly with short steps, especially because you are in a hurry.
8 To pull something, especially with a sudden movement, in order to remove it.
9 To lower oneself onto one's knees.
10 To walk or move with a lack of balance as if you are going to fall.
11 To risk going somewhere or doing something that might be dangerous or unpleasant, or to risk saying something that might be criticized.
13 To press something into a smaller space.
15 To disappear suddenly.
16 If something _____s you, it is so confusing that you cannot understand it.
18 More difficult or sever than usual.

Comprehension Quiz Answers

Ch 1	1. C-B-D-A 2. B 3. C-A-B-D 4. C 5. C 6. A
Ch 2	1. A-d, B-c 2. B, D 3. D 4. D 5. A, B
Ch 3	1. C 2. B-A-D-C 3. B 4. C 5. A 6. C
Ch 4	1. B 2. B, D 3. C 4. 4, 3, 2, 1 5. B
Ch 5	1. C 2. B, D 3. C 4. A
Ch 6	1. D 2. B 3. A, B 4. B 5. B
Ch 7	1. C 2. D 3. D 4. B 5. B, C
Ch 8	1. C 2. A 3. A, D 4. D 5. A-2, B-1, C-4, D-3
Ch 9	1. A 2. A 3. C 4. D 5. A, B
Ch 10	1. D 2. B, D 3. C 4. C 5. A
Ch 11	1. A, D 2. B 3. D 4. The cake was fully 18 inches in diameter. 5. A-D-C-B
Ch 12	1. B 2. D 3. C 4. To put a newt in the water to scare the Trunchbull.
Ch 13	1. A, C 2. They learn a little song that teaches the spelling. 3. D 4. D 5. C 6. They are all crooked.
Ch 14	1. A, C 2. B 3. D 4. C 5. D
Ch 15	1. C 2. B, D 3. D 4. B

Ch 16   1. A, C   2. C   3. C   4. (A)In the well   5. (A) poor

Ch 17   1. A-D-B-C   2. For two years   3. Her aunt raised her and wants to be repaid for the food and clothes that she bought for Miss Honey.   4. C   5. C

Ch 18   (No Questions)

Ch 19   1. C   2. It was hard   3. B, D   4. A-(F), B-(T), C-(T)   5. B

Ch 20   1. B   2. C   3. A-C-D-B

Ch 21   1. Mr. Trilby became the new headmaster.   2. She was moved to the top form.   3. C   4. D-A-C-B   5. C, D   6. B

Crossword Puzzle Answers(Ch 1-4)

Across

4 formidable
9 instinctive
11 crawl
14 revolt
16 seize
17 crouch
18 unbearable

Down

1 doting
2 enormous
3 scarce
5 applaud
6 spoil
7 nimble
8 rattle
10 extraordinary
11 convince
12 suspicion
13 flick
15 wreck

Crossword Puzzle Answers (Ch 5-8)

Across

3 adore
4 splendid
5 incapable
6 purposely
8 scorch
12 coarse
14 crop
17 reluctantly
19 formidable

Down

1 fragile
2 precious
7 snort
9 hunk
10 possess
11 menace
13 devour
15 quiver
16 stink
18 tip

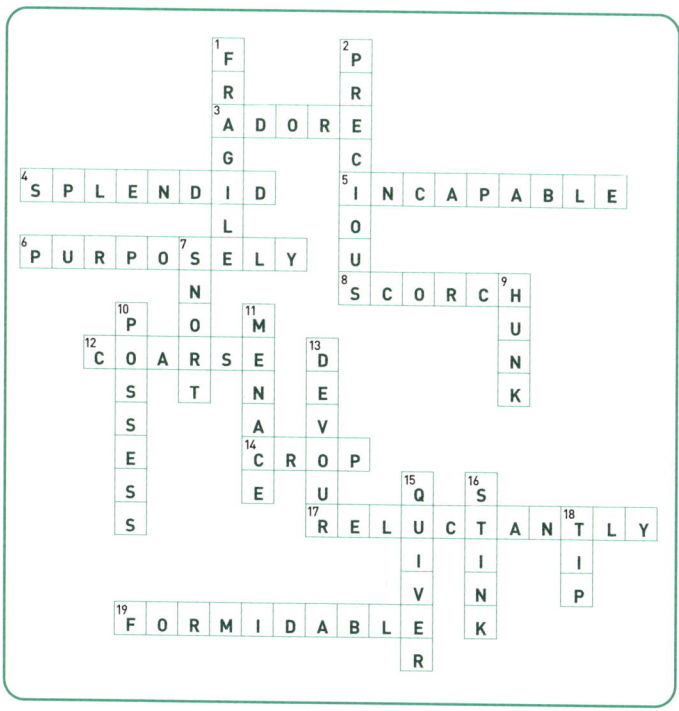

Crossword Puzzle Answers(Ch 9-12)

Across

3 mumble
5 peculiar
6 blur
8 gallant
12 surrender
13 totter
17 stutter
18 presume
19 subtle

Down

1 swear
2 belch
3 murky
4 exploit
7 culprit
9 lunge
10 crafty
11 stagger
14 tense
15 startle
16 froth

Crossword Puzzle Answers (Ch 13-16)

Across

3 ignorant
5 froth
7 crumbly
8 astound
10 conceit
12 crook
15 spur
16 infuriate
17 blithe
18 assemble
19 topple

Down

1 peculiar
2 fraction
4 appall
6 cluster
9 duck
11 teeter
12 compel
13 wriggle
14 tremble

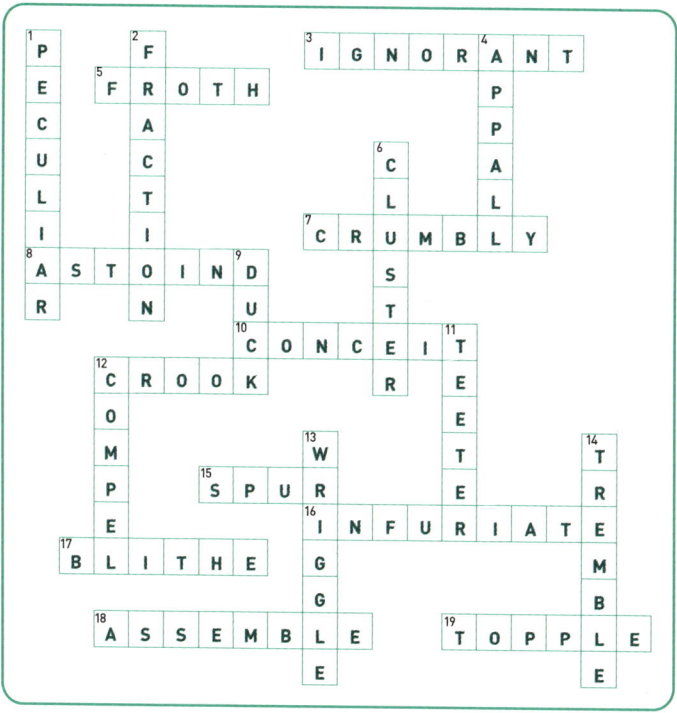

Crossword Puzzle Answers(Ch 17-21)

Across

3 ponder
6 mumble
7 scorch
12 fluster
14 consent
17 sip
19 tragedy
20 confront
21 fiercely

Down

1 seize
2 reassemble
4 stare
5 authority
7 scurry
8 pluck
9 kneel
10 stagger
11 venture
13 compress
15 vanish
16 bewilder
18 stiff

Matilda를 완독하셨군요! 축하합니다!

로알드 달의 다른 책도 꾸준히 읽어보세요.

Matilda를 재미있게 읽으셨다면 Roald Dahl의 다른 대표작인 Chalie and the Chocolate Factory와 James and the Giant Peach도 함께 읽어보세요. 같은 저자의 시리즈를 읽다보면 비슷한 문체와 어휘를 반복해서 만나게 되고, 이는 리딩 속도 향상과 어휘력 신장으로 자연스레 이어집니다. Chalie and the Chocolate Factory와 James and the Giant Peach의 『원서 읽는 단어장』은 시중 서점 및 인터넷 서점에서 구입할 수 있습니다. 인터넷 서점에서 '원서 읽는 단어장'을 검색해보세요.

무료 단어장을 받아보세요!

다른 원서를 읽을 때도 정리된 단어장이 있다면 정말 좋겠지요? www.readingtc.com/voca를 방문해보세요. 원서별로 어려운 어휘를 정리한 단어장 무료 PDF를 제공하고 있습니다.

모든 원서들의 단어장을 제공하고 있진 못하지만, 비교적 많이 읽히는 원서를 중심으로 꾸준히 업데이트 되고 있습니다. 새로운 원서를 읽기 전에 단어장이 준비되어 있지는 않은가 꼭 한번 확인해보세요!

함께 모여 원서 읽는 〈스피드 리딩 카페〉

어떤 원서를 읽을지 고민이신가요? 원서를 꾸준히 읽고 싶은데 잘 안 되시나요? 그럴 때는 함께 모여 원서를 읽는 〈스피드 리딩 카페 cafe.naver.com/readingtc〉를 방문해보세요. 수준별 추천 원서 목록, 함께 만든 원서별 단어장, 매월 진행되는 북클럽 등 원서 읽기에 도움이 되는 자료가 넘쳐납니다. 무엇보다 원서를 함께 읽을 동료들을 만날 수 있는 멋진 곳이랍니다! 이미 수천 명이 함께 모여 원서를 읽고 있지요. 원서 읽기에 관심이 있으시다면 이곳을 방문해서 함께 참여해보세요!

원서 읽는 단어장

Matilda

1판 1쇄 2009년 2월 23일
1판 20쇄 2025년 9월 2일

기획 이수영
책임편집 김수진
콘텐츠 제작 롱테일 교육 연구소
마케팅 두잉글 사업본부

펴낸이 이수영
펴낸곳 롱테일북스
출판등록 제2015-000191호
주소 04033 서울특별시 마포구 양화로 113, 3층(서교동, 순흥빌딩)
전자메일 help@ltinc.net

이 도서는 대한민국에서 제작되었습니다.

ISBN 978-89-5605-329-5 14740
      978-89-5605-319-6 (세트)